The rebord
America :
2003.

THE REBORDERING
OF NORTH AMERICA

THE REBORDERING
OF NORTH AMERICA

Integration and Exclusion in a
New Security Context

EDITED BY

PETER ANDREAS AND
THOMAS J. BIERSTEKER

Routledge
NEW YORK AND LONDON

Published in 2003 by
Routledge
29 West 35th Street
New York, NY 10001
www.routledge-ny.com

Published in Great Britain by
Routledge
11 New Fetter Lane
London EC4P 4EE
www.routledge.co.uk

Library of Congress Cataloging-in-Publication Data

The rebordering of North America : integration and exclusion in a new security context / edited by Peter Andreas and Thomas J. Biersteker.
    p.   cm.
    Includes bibliographical references and index.
    ISBN 0-415-94466-X (alk. paper)—ISBN 0-415-94467-8 (pbk. : alk. paper)
    1. United States–Relations–Canada.   2. United States–Relations–Mexico.
3. Canada–Relations–United States.   4. Mexico–Relations–United States.
5. National security–United States.   6. Border patrols–United States.   7. War on Terrorism, 2001—Influence.   I. Andreas, Peter, 1965–   II. Biersteker, Thomas J.

E183.8.C2R395 2003
363.3′2′0973—dc21   2003005291

CONTENTS

A TALE OF TWO BORDERS

The U.S.-Canada and U.S.-Mexico Lines after 9-11

PETER ANDREAS

The conventional wisdom in recent years has been that "globalization" is about breaking down borders.[1] Indeed, we are often told that growing economic integration and interdependence leads to a retreat of the regulatory state, more open borders, and more harmonious cross-border relations. Prominent free market advocates, such as the *Wall Street Journal*,[2] have even pushed to make borders not only more meaningless for the flow of goods and money but also for people, giving substance to the upbeat business school rhetoric of an emerging "borderless world."[3] President Vicente Fox of Mexico epitomized this view at the regional level when he entered office by promoting a bold vision of an open U.S.-Mexico border, including the free movement of labor, and the creation of a North American community. Such a vision would further deepen an already well-advanced continental integration process: The U.S.-Canada and U.S.-Mexico borders are the two busiest land crossings in the world, with cross-border commercial flows accelerating sharply since the launching of the North American Free Trade Agreement (NAFTA).[4]

Fox's border-free vision of North America was one of the first casualties of the devastating terrorist attacks on the Twin Towers and the Pentagon on September 11, 2001. In both political debates and policy practice, borders are very much back in style. Rather than simply being dismantled in the face of intensifying pressures of economic integration, border controls are being retooled and redesigned as part of a new and expanding "war on terrorism." The immediate U.S. response to the terrorist attacks included a dramatic tightening of border inspections and a toughening of the policy discourse about borders and cross-border flows. The political scramble to "do something" about leaky borders has slowed and complicated North American economic integration. Traditional border issues such as trade and migration are now inescapably evaluated through a security lens. Optimistic talk of opening borders has been replaced by more anxious and somber talk about "security perimeters" and "homeland defense." Not surprisingly, politicians from across the political spectrum have been rushing to demonstrate their commitment to securing borders.[5] At least for the time being, talking about open borders is considered politically impolite. Indeed, the voices for breaking down borders are not only muted but also attacked and ostracized by their political opponents.[6] Terrorism has predictably heightened the American public's awareness of and fears about porous borders: According to a Zogby public opinion survey a few weeks after the terrorist attacks, 72 percent of those polled said better border controls and stricter enforcement of immigration laws would help prevent terrorism.[7]

This is the first book that evaluates the implications of September 11 and the new "war on terrorism" for border controls, cross-border relations, and economic integration in North America. More generally, the book contributes to ongoing scholarly and policy discussions over the meaning and management of borders in a rapidly changing world, and adds fuel to broader debates over the shifting nature of borders and territorial politics in a new security environment. The book crosses both professional and geographic borders, bringing together leading scholars and policy analysts from Canada, Mexico, and the United States. They examine U.S.-Canada and U.S.-Mexico relations in the wake of the terrorist attacks, the management of trade and migration flows, and the reconceptualization of North America's borders in the post–9-11 world.

The book's contributors address several key questions of interest to both the academic and policy communities in North America: In what ways has continental integration been derailed or reinforced by the terrorist attacks and the new primacy of security? How are the regulatory border apparatuses of the NAFTA partners being retooled and reconfigured in response to terrorism? What are the obstacles to creating a more efficient and effective system for regulating cross-border flows?

In an era of heightened anxiety over border security, can security be enhanced without undermining legitimate cross-border trade and travel? If so, how? What are the limits and opportunities for cross-border cooperation, and how are these similar or different in the U.S.-Canada and the U.S.-Mexico relationships? Given the asymmetrical nature of economic interdependence between the United States and Canada and between the United States and Mexico, does cross-border collaboration and policy harmonization simply mean conforming to U.S. policy preferences? Do the post–9-11 policy initiatives to date reflect a multilateral construction of a North American security community, a unilateral building of a fortress America with buffer states to the north and south, or something else? The book's authors tackle these difficult and complex questions from a variety of analytical perspectives, disciplinary approaches, and national backgrounds.[8] They do not provide uniform answers but do share an intense concern for the future of North America and the direction of the continental integration process.

In this introductory chapter, I trace the changing practice and politics of North American border controls and analyze the implications of these changes for cross-border relations and continental integration. More than ever, I suggest, North American relations are driven by the politics of border control. I first examine U.S. border control initiatives before 9-11 and argue that these were politically successful policy failures: They succeeded in terms of their symbolic and image effects even while largely failing in terms of their deterrent effects. I then highlight the border-related economic, bureaucratic, and political repercussions of 9-11. I show why the task of border control has become more difficult, cumbersome, and disruptive in the post–9-11 era, with significant ramifications for the North American integration project. I conclude by outlining three possible future border trajectories and provide a brief preview of the rest of the book.

U.S. Border Controls before 9-11

The post–9-11 U.S. campaign to secure its borders is in some respects reminiscent of the 1990s when an anti-immigration backlash fueled an unprecedented border crackdown along the U.S.-Mexico line. High-profile enforcement campaigns such as "Operation Gatekeeper" south

of San Diego and "Operation Hold-the-Line" in El Paso helped pro-
pel a rapid expansion of the Immigration and Naturalization Service
(INS). Since the early 1990s, the INS budget has more than tripled,
making it the fastest growing federal agency. More INS agents are now
authorized to carry a gun than any other federal law enforcement force.
Today, there are more Border Patrol agents (the uniformed enforcement wing of the INS) in the San Diego sector alone than there were
along the entire 2,000–mile–long southwest border two decades ago.
The southern U.S. border was also partly militarized through the "war
on drugs," with the military drafted to play an interdiction support
role. At the same time, as policymakers were attempting to make the
border more secure, they were also making it more business-friendly
to accommodate the requirements of NAFTA. The seemingly paradoxical end result was the construction of both a borderless economy
and a barricaded border.[9] The border had become both more blurred
and more sharply demarcated than ever before.

This pre–9-11 U.S. border enforcement build-up, overwhelmingly
focused on drugs and illegal immigration, can be characterized as a
politically successful policy failure.[10] It was a policy failure since it did
not significantly deter the unauthorized flow of drugs and people into
the United States. In the case of immigration control, the resident
unauthorized immigrant population actually has doubled since 1990
to roughly 8 million people. For the most part, high-profile border
enforcement campaigns did more to redirect rather than reduce the
flow of unauthorized migrants. In the case of drug control, intensified
border interdiction had little effect on curbing drug imports, with the
availability of drugs such as cocaine and heroin as high as ever (and at
lower prices and higher purity levels). At best, the enforcement crackdown affected the methods and specific locations of drug trafficking
across the border, but without a noticeable reduction in the overall
supply.

Moreover, the border enforcement campaign was a policy failure not
only because it proved to be a poor deterrent, but also because it had
a number of perverse and counterproductive consequences. For example, the border crackdown fueled the emergence of more skilled and
sophisticated transnational migrant smuggling groups, creating a more
serious organized crime problem along and across the border. Drug

smugglers also responded to law enforcement pressure by integrating more with legitimate cargo. They used the NAFTA-encouraged boom in trade to more effectively camouflage their illicit shipments. One negative unintended result was the creation of closer ties between licit and illicit trade. After years of intensified enforcement, the tasks of drug and immigration control at the border had actually become harder. New law enforcement initiatives were systematically countered by new law evasion techniques. Tragically, this included turning to the use of more remote and dangerous entry points in the deserts and mountains for migrant smuggling, leading to hundreds of migrant deaths every year.[11] An average of two migrants have died each day in the past two years while attempting to cross the border.[12]

These border policy failures and perverse consequences nevertheless can be viewed as politically successful for a variety of reasons. The high visibility of the border campaigns generated substantial political and bureaucratic rewards. For example, even if the overall level of unauthorized immigration did not decline, the border crackdown made key urban entry points appear much more "under control." Illegal crossers were pushed out of sight (into more remote deserts and mountains) and therefore out of the media spotlight and the public's mind. This, in turn, helped to neutralize political opponents and muffled the substantial anti-illegal-immigration backlash that had built up in the early 1990s, especially in places such as southern California. Continued border arrests and seizures also provided border enforcers with ready-made (if highly imperfect and misleading) visible indicators of government progress and commitment to creating a more orderly border. This helped win votes for politicians and secure higher budgets for enforcement bureaucracies. One of the Border Patrol's biggest problems was adjusting to its fast-paced growth and hiring enough new agents to keep up with congressionally mandated staffing increases. Importantly, the expected level of deterrence was actually modest. Those charged with the task of border drug interdiction, for example, never claimed that they were stopping more than a small percentage of drug shipments. Similarly, even while boasting that the border was more "under control," the INS acknowledged that the unauthorized immigrant population in the country continued to grow at a rapid pace. What seemed to matter most to politicians and bureaucrats was the high visibility and symbolic value of the border deterrence effort, and that they could point to indicators showing "progress" toward the goal of border security.

Equally important, the U.S. border control offensive was carried out without substantially impeding the enormous (and rapidly growing) volume of legitimate cross-border flows. Each year, some 300 million people, 90 million cars, and 4.3 million trucks cross into the United States from Mexico, reflecting an increasingly integrated and interdependent region. Trade flows between the two nations have more than tripled during the past decade, from $81 billion in 1993 to $247 billion in 2000, mostly in products moved across the border by truck.[13] During this mushrooming of trade, border law enforcement never trumped the facilitation of legitimate border crossings. Border wait times for vehicles and pedestrians were, for the most part, manageable and tolerable. At some key border crossings, such as at the San Ysidro port of entry south of San Diego, border wait times actually decreased in the 1990s. To accommodate the growth in crossings, ten new ports of entry have been built since the start of NAFTA, bringing the total along the border to fifty. In short, even as the U.S.-Mexico border appeared to be a more impressively policed barrier, it also became a busier and more business-friendly bridge.

U.S. Border Controls after 9-11

Since the terrorist attacks on September 11, business as usual at the border has been much less tolerable. In the new and expanding counterterrorism effort, the expectation of success is significantly higher than in the cases of drug and immigration control—indeed, the deterrence level is expected to be an impossible 100 percent. Yet the mission is clearly far more difficult: If the existing border enforcement apparatus has proven unable to stop multi-ton shipments of drugs and hundreds of thousands of crossings by unauthorized migrants every year, the chances of deterring a few bombs or terrorists is far more remote. Moreover, the handy visible indicators of progress traditionally used for border enforcement work (and which are crucial in the annual process of justifying agency budgets) are not as applicable and available. Counterterrorism "successes" are less frequent, less visible, and more secretive. In short, border enforcers have been given a harder job, face higher expectations for success, and cannot rely on the same old convenient measures of progress.

Facing intense political pressure and public scrutiny, border strategists have been trying to take the old drug and immigration enforcement infrastructure and quickly adapt it to the counterterrorism effort. It is an awkward and cumbersome fit. The INS enforcement apparatus was designed to handle millions of migrant workers entering the country in search of employment rather than to detect and deter those few determined individuals who arrive to commit terrorist acts. Counterterrorism has been traditionally a low priority for the INS. Similarly, the U.S. Customs Service had until September 2001 been focused on drug control, and along the coastlines, the U.S. Coast Guard has focused its energies on interdicting drugs and illegal migrants. These already overwhelmed enforcement agencies are now forced to reinvent themselves for the post–9-11 world. While they face unreasonably high public expectations for success, they are at the same time the recipients of substantial new resources.

The FY 2003 budget provides more than a $2 billion increase in border security funding. This includes a 29 percent increase in the budget of the INS, a 36 percent increase in the inspections budget of the Customs Service, and the largest budget increase in the Coast Guard's history. A more radical transformation in the works is not simply more resources, but a consolidation and reorganization of various agencies under a new Department of Homeland Security representing the largest reorganization of the federal government in half a century. Under the current plan, the new department will bring together parts of many existing departments and agencies, including the Coast Guard, Customs Service, and the INS. This reorganization reflects the growing prominence of law enforcement in national security institutions and missions, and a further blurring of the traditional distinction between internal and external security threats.[14]

Another striking departure from earlier U.S. border control campaigns is that this time much of the political heat from Washington is focused not only on a different worry (terrorism), but also on a border that has long been conveniently kept out of the political spotlight:

the U.S.-Canada border. While there has been considerable clandestine cross-border activity along the northern U.S. border,[15] this has
remained largely under the political radar screen as American border anxieties have been directed southward. Historically, the United
States has had the luxury of largely forgetting about its northern border, which Canadians used to complain about, but in retrospect had
certain advantages (the only thing worse than no attention is negative
attention). The openness of the border, labeled "the world's longest
undefended border," traditionally has been a source of mutual pride,
but is now perceived and treated as a source of vulnerability by the
United States.[16] Even though none of the nineteen hijackers involved
in the September 11 attacks entered across the border and in fact had
been issued visas by the United States, some U.S. media reports have
depicted Canada as a haven for terrorists who exploit Canada's liberal
refugee and immigration system.[17] (Canada, unlike the United States,
does not detain asylum seekers. Some 10,000 fail to show up for their
scheduled hearings every year and simply disappear.)[18]

Since 9-11, Canada has been receiving a heavy dose of the harsh
scrutiny the United States usually reserves for Mexico on border-
related law enforcement issues. Canada has suddenly found itself in
the highly uncomfortable and unfamiliar position of being perceived
and treated as a security risk. Barely policed—only 334 agents police
the northern border, compared to more than 9,000 agents assigned
to police the U.S.–Mexico border—the U.S.–Canada border is an easy
and convenient political target for those who blame lax border controls
for the country's vulnerability to terrorism.

The Border Patrol hiring boom during the past decade, which more
than doubled the size of the force, was almost exclusively directed
at the U.S.-Mexico border. On September 11, there were as many
Border Patrol agents in Brownsville, Texas, as there were on the entire
U.S.-Canada border.[19] Senator Byron Dorgan (D-ND) held up a rub-
ber cone at a congressional hearing on northern border security in late
2001 to show what meets foreigners who arrive at some checkpoints
after 10:00 p.m.: "This is America's security at our border crossings. It
is not enough," he said. "America can't effectively combat terrorism if
it doesn't control its borders."[20] Remove the word "terrorism" and put
in the words "drug trafficking" or "illegal immigration" and the new

discourse of border security is strikingly familiar, mimicking the older discourse that has characterized U.S. border relations with Mexico. In this sense, there has been a Mexicanization of U.S.-Canada border politics.

One of the many new measures Congress has pushed through as part of the Patriot Act is a tripling of agents deployed to the northern border. National Guard troops have also been sent to help with patrols and inspections at border posts. The Coast Guard now stops all boats crossing the Great Lakes and escorts gas and oil tankers. As welcome as these deployments may be, given that a far more substantial U.S. law enforcement force along the U.S.-Mexico border has failed to deter hundreds of thousands of illegal border crossings each year, there is little reason to believe that a much smaller force along the far longer northern border can somehow keep out a handful of determined terrorists. Beefing up personnel on the U.S.-Canada border is therefore likely to have little more than a placebo effect (however important that may be for domestic political consumption).

The U.S. Customs Service traditionally has been able to inspect only a fraction of total incoming trade, and thus doubling or even tripling the amount of cargo inspected would not significantly enhance security. And even if key border crossing points, such as between Detroit and Windsor, Ontario (27 percent of U.S.-Canada trade crosses the Ambassador Bridge alone[21]), could be fully secured somehow, this still leaves thousands of miles of the border essentially wide open. The U.S.-Canada border commonly has been described as a border with many gates and no fences.

While a sustained enforcement crackdown at U.S. land ports of entry may help to reassure and calm a nervous public, in practice it may do more to inhibit legitimate travel and trade than terrorists. Security, in other words, has become a new kind of trade barrier. As Stephen Flynn notes, the U.S. border security response immediately following the September attacks was the equivalent of the world's most powerful country imposing a trade embargo on itself.[22] More intensive border inspections have had serious economic repercussions along both the U.S.-Mexico and U.S.-Canada borders.

After the September 11 attacks, U.S. border inspectors were put on a level 1 Alert, defined as a "sustained, intensive, antiterrorism operation." The predictable result was a dramatic slowing of cross-border traffic. The United States and Canada conduct $1.3 billion worth of two-way trade a day, most of which is moved by truck across the border.[23] Some 40,000 commercial shipments and 300,000 people cross the 4,000–mile–long U.S.-Canada border every day. In the days after the attacks, delays for trucks hauling cargo across the border increased from 1–2 minutes to 10–15 hours, stranding parts, shipments, and perishable goods. For example, trucks were backed up for 36 kilometers at the Ambassador Bridge linking Windsor, Ontario and Detroit. Before 9-11, trucks with preclearance could often cross the border in 1–2 minutes.[24] The auto industry was particularly hard hit by the post–9-11 border delays. According to Mark Nantis of the Canadian Vehicle Manufacturers Association, "The unplanned production loss resulting from parts shortages cost manufacturing facilities approximately $1 million to $1.5 million [Canadian dollars] per hour...." Due to post–9-11 parts shortages, Ford closed an engine plant in Windsor and a vehicle plant in Michigan.[25]

Massive traffic jams and long delays also characterized the U.S.-Mexico border. Cross-border trade between the United States and Mexico has skyrocketed in the past decade, and most of this trade is transported by truck through the major border ports of entry. The high-intensity border checks following the bombings put a noticeable brake on cross-border flows. In Laredo, Texas, for example, during peak crossing times before the attacks, it took about five minutes for a pedestrian to cross a bridge checkpoint and a half hour for a motorist. Immediately after the attacks, the wait increased up to five hours. Officials counted 2.9 million people entering Laredo from Mexico in September 2001—down from 3.5 million in September 2000.[26] Retail sales in U.S. border cities immediately plummeted as Mexican shoppers stayed south of the border. San Diego declared a state of economic emergency due to the business downturn after September 11. Mexican border towns were similarly shaken by a sharp drop in U.S. visitors (with the notable exception being a rush of U.S. shoppers buying large quantities of Cipro, an antibiotic to treat anthrax infection). Cross-border trade, which had been running at about $670 million, fell by an average of 15 percent in the weeks following the attacks. Most severely affected were electronics, textiles, chemicals, and Mexican factories supplying just-in-time parts to U.S. auto companies.

In short, while the process of North American integration has not been reversed, it has been slowed and complicated by a U.S. law enforcement squeeze on the cross-border transportation arteries that provide its life-blood. While border delays are not as long now as they were immediately following the terrorist attacks, more intensive inspections have continued to have a chilling effect on cross-border exchange. Balancing the twin policy objectives of border facilitation and enforcement has always been an awkward task. But with the terrorism threat placed at the top of an already overextended border control agenda, the balancing act has become far more cumbersome and difficult.

Before 9-11, the coping strategy was to stress visible symbolic measures that projected an image of heightened security, while making sure not to slow legitimate cross-border flows. Political tolerance for such a strategy is now much lower. In the current high anxiety climate, those charged with the task of managing borders are expected to prioritize security, even while the sheer magnitude of border crossings limit how much borders can be secured effectively. The increasingly favored coping mechanism has been to emphasize new cargo tracking systems, inspection technologies, and innovative traffic management strategies to ease border congestion and enhance security at the same time. This was clearly articulated in the thirty-point "smart border" declaration signed between Canada and the United States in December 2001, and partially extended to the U.S.-Mexico border the following spring.[27]

Canada and Mexico: Two Scared Mice Next to a Neurotic Elephant[28]

The need to keep the U.S.-Canada and U.S.-Mexico borders open for business also has placed enormous pressure on Canada and Mexico to beef up their own counterterrorism efforts. Canada and Mexico are discovering the high price of asymmetric interdependence. While all three North American countries benefit from a close economic relationship, Canada and Mexico are far more reliant on trade with the United States than the other way around and are therefore much more vulnerable to disruptions in cross-border commercial flows. For example, while about 25 percent of U.S. trade goes to Canada, 87 percent of Canada's trade is U.S.-bound. Equally important, foreign trade represents a much greater percentage of the Canadian economy than it does of the American economy. Forty percent of Canada's GDP depends on exports to the United States, while only 2.5 percent of U.S. GDP is tied to exports to Canada.[29] The imbalance is even more evident in the U.S.-Mexico trading relationship: Almost 90 percent of Mexico's trade goes to the United States, while only 15 percent of U.S. exports go to Mexico. This structural asymmetry gives Washington significant policy leverage over its immediate neighbors, leaving them with limited space to maneuver. Here the United States largely sets the policy agenda and narrows the room for autonomous policy choices.[30] In this precarious context, Canada and Mexico are like two scared mice next to a neurotic elephant. They are more worried about the elephant's reaction to terrorism than about terrorism itself. In the effort to cope pragmatically with this unstable and unpredictable new policy environment, the two mice are trying to convince the elephant that they are part of the solution rather than part of the problem.

Thus, in the immediate aftermath of the terrorist attacks, the Mexican government detained and questioned hundreds of people of Middle-Eastern origin, restricted the entry of citizens from a number of Central Asian and Middle Eastern countries, and provided U.S. authorities with intelligence information on possible suspects based in Mexico. President Fox has proposed a new intelligence-gathering law to Congress and has offered to target bank accounts of suspected terrorists. A new security outfit of Israeli- and U.S.-trained border enforcers is reportedly being sent to replace immigration officials in the southern border state of Chiapas. Mexico also is creating a national immigration database, and is upgrading computers and setting up new false document detectors at southern border checkpoints.[31] It seems that Mexico has pragmatically accepted that part of the price of being viewed and treated as an insider, rather than as an outsider, is to police more intensively its southern border. Central American neighbors, in turn, complain that a hardening of Mexico's southern border means

Mexico is doing Washington's police work. Indeed, Mexico's border enforcement initiatives may be viewed as a "thickening" of the U.S. border, with Mexico becoming a buffer zone.

For Mexico, the new politics of fighting terrorism in some respects resembles the older and more familiar politics of fighting drugs. While Mexico no doubt welcomes less U.S. scrutiny and diplomatic arm-twisting on drug control issues after 9-11, there are heightened pressures and expectations to contribute to U.S. anti-terrorism goals. As in the anti-drug effort, Mexico is expected to demonstrate its resolve and cooperation in meeting U.S. law enforcement objectives. While certainly not uncontroversial in Mexican domestic politics, the new antiterrorism mission provides a less diplomatically sensitive impetus for cross-border security cooperation than has been the case with drug control. It also provides a more politically palatable rationale for Mexico to cooperate on immigration control (as long as it is directed at non-Mexican nationals).[32] The Fox government is careful to characterize terrorism as a mutual security concern, and in a sharp departure from past official rhetoric, even talks about security as an "interdependent matter."[33]

In exchange for greater cooperation on the anti-terrorism front, Mexico wants to assure not only unimpeded commerce across the Rio Grande, but also has continued to aggressively push for a migration deal with Washington that would include regularizing the status of some 3.5 million unauthorized Mexican workers in the United States. In the summer of 2001, the Fox administration had high hopes of reaching a migration agreement, only to have this placed on the political backburner after the terrorist attacks. Even before 9-11, this was going to be a tough sell in Washington, with policymakers deeply divided on the issue. The terrorist attacks and subsequent mobilization for the antiterrorism campaign provided President Bush with a convenient excuse to put negotiations over such a delicate and sensitive issue on hold. Thus, the political momentum that had been building up in Mexico's favor, including a softening of the U.S. immigration debate, was reversed in the wake of 9-11.

On the Canadian side, Ottawa has taken many measures since September 11 to demonstrate its resolve against terrorism and heightened commitment to border security.[34] It immediately put into place a high state of alert at border crossings, enhanced the levels of security at the country's airports, added $176 million ($280 million in Canadian dollars) in new funding for detection technologies and personnel to strengthen the security framework,[35] initiated new legislation to combat the financing of terrorism, and froze the assets of known terrorist groups.[36] Some 2,000 officers of the Royal Canadian Mounted Police have been reassigned to border patrol and anti-terrorism work. To counter the image that Canada is lax on immigration controls, the government has introduced a permanent fraud-resistant resident card for new immigrants, increased its detention capacity and deportation activity, and conducted more front-end security screening for refugee claimants.[37] Canada has also tightened its visa regime, including requiring Saudi and Malaysian visitors to obtain visas.

For domestic political reasons, Canadian officials are careful to emphasize that these measures do not mean Canada is simply adopting U.S. policies or conforming to pressures from Washington. But the political incentives are obvious: Either take strong measures to enhance security or risk a unilateral hardening of the border.[38] Canadians interpreted a post–9-11 warning by Secretary of State Colin Powell as a thinly veiled threat: "Some nations need to be more vigilant against terrorism at their borders if they want their relationship with the U.S. to remain the same."[39] While Canadian officials are wary of talking about creating a "security perimeter"[40] (preferring instead the softer, less militaristic term "zone of confidence"), both the government and the business community[41] recognize the high stakes and have single-mindedly mobilized around the task of assuring smooth-flowing ports of entry along the border. Their economic survival depends on it.[42]

Future Border Trajectories

Given the current conditions of high uncertainty, it would be premature, indeed reckless, to try to predict the future of borders and border controls in the NAFTA zone. Nevertheless, three potential trajectories can be briefly outlined. At one extreme is a unilateral fortification and hardening of U.S. border defenses (a "fortress America"), with security trumping all other considerations. This radical option runs counter to powerful economic interests, and indeed the business communities in all three North American countries have mobilized since 9-11 to try to avoid precisely this outcome. At the other extreme are multilateral policy harmonization and a "pooling" of sovereignty to build a formal North American security perimeter (a "fortress North America").

Such a path would represent a Europeanization of border controls and thus a qualitative transformation of the continental integration project. As part of the process of dismantling borders within the European Union (EU) and creating a shared economic space of free movement, EU members have built up a common external perimeter through the Schengen Agreement.[43] This includes common visa and asylum policies, a shared information system, and standardized border procedures. Brussels is even contemplating the creation of a joint corps of EU border guards to patrol the outer perimeter.[44]

To "Schengenize" North America's borders in a similar manner would require a level of formal institutionalization and policy harmonization that is difficult to imagine in the present context, and only sustained shocks, such as multiple large-scale terrorist incidents, would create the political will necessary to push in this direction.[45] Interestingly, Mexico has been the biggest proponent of this approach to North American security, with Canada being the most resistant.[46] Based on current trends, the most likely scenario falls somewhere in the middle, neither a "fortress America" nor a full-scale, institutionalized "fortress North America" project, but rather a series of incremental, piecemeal initiatives, involving a mixture of enhanced cross-border security coordination and collaboration, partial and uneven policy convergence, and innovative new inspection methods and technologies that increasingly extend beyond the ports of entry ("smart borders").[47] This may eventually develop into a less formal, less bureaucratized, quasi-continental security perimeter that selectively borrows from the European model.

Obviously the particular direction taken will greatly depend on the location, method, timing, intensity, and frequency of any future terrorist incidents. It is important to note that while the hijackings on 9-11 were not directly linked to the U.S.-Mexico or U.S.-Canada borders, they nevertheless had dramatic, ripple effects on the borders. A more directly border-related incident, such as terrorists entering the country across the U.S.-Mexico or U.S.-Canada borders, or a bomb exploding that had been smuggled through a border port of entry, would likely generate far more intensive calls for hardening borders. If sustained, a high-intensity border crackdown could potentially stall and even derail the continental economic integration process. There is nothing automatic about the policy reaction to any future attacks. The politics of the policy response matter as much as any actual attack. Beyond the actual levels of destruction and disruption that such future terrorist events may cause, U.S. images and perceptions of its NAFTA partners will be crucial. Amongst the many political choices will be whether (and to what extent) American policymakers point an accusatory finger northward and/or southward. Post–9-11 Canadian and Mexican policy initiatives should be viewed as trust- and confidence-building measures designed to inhibit such a response.

A Brief Preview of the Chapters Ahead

In the next chapter, Athanasios Hristoulas analyzes one of the more striking ironies of post–9-11 North American politics: Canada and Mexico have in some respects traded places in their official policy stance. On the one hand, Mexico, with a well-established tradition of independence in the making of foreign security policy, has enthusiastically encouraged the development of a multilateral security mechanism. On the other hand, Canada, which historically has stressed multilateralism in foreign security policy, has so far largely rejected a multilateral approach to North American security. Hristoulas explores these contrasting positions, explaining why Mexico has pushed to trilateralize continental policy initiatives while Canada has attempted to avoid it.[48]

Mónica Serrano's chapter examines how security cooperation worked in the past between Mexico and the United States, and why it has unraveled so rapidly just when it is most needed. Although after 9-11 we might have expected the security alliance to really take off, instead the foreign policy aspirations of the Fox administration have been pricked by the realities of a domestic politics for which newly stringent U.S. policies have an immediately negative cultural resonance in Mexico. Rather than cooperation, Serrano emphasizes that backlash and conflict seem to be again winning the day in U.S.-Mexico relations.

The next two chapters focus our attention on Canadian politics, the U.S.-Canada border, and U.S.-Canadian relations. Stephen Clarkson examines how the "terrorist coup" of September 11 transformed Canadians' consciousness of their position in North America. Having prided themselves on their increased trade and investment integration in the continental economy, Clarkson notes that Canadians suddenly found that they were exposed to the consequences of extreme dependence. The U.S. self-blockade along its borders in the immediate aftermath of 9-11 caused a panic within a business community dependent on just-in-time, cross-border production. Ottawa quickly reoriented itself from national development schemes to satisfying Washington that its security measures were trustworthy. Clarkson concludes that the Canadian government now finds itself living less in fear of Al Qaeda than of Uncle Sam's reactions to Al Qaeda. Far from delivering a new stability, he stresses that trade liberalization has produced new uncertainties.

Louis Pauly's chapter critically evaluates Canada's domestic political debate over the implications of 9-11 for Canada and U.S.-Canadian relations. He emphasizes that heightened perceptions of asymmetric economic and security interdependence are transforming Canada's political and policy landscape, giving greater influence and voice to pragmatic policymakers who are willing and able to make considerable compromises on border-related questions. As a result, a new, pragmatic vision of Canada, the border, and U.S.-Canadian relations has confronted an emotionally charged nationalist one at the federal level. Although the situation remains in flux and it is too early to predict with great certainty, Pauly expects the pragmatists to ultimately win out, with important political consequences for Canada and the U.S.-Canadian relationship.

Stephen Flynn's chapter argues for a fundamental rethinking of how to regulate cross-border flows in North America. According to Flynn, developing the means to manage the "transnational muck" that is contaminating the integrative process along the U.S.-Mexico and U.S.-Canada borders is essential, but we need to liberate ourselves from the notion that borders are the best place to do this. He demonstrates that an overreliance on borders to regulate and police the flow of goods and people can perversely contribute to the problem. Flynn explores how efforts to promote security throughout the trade corridor, as opposed to placing primary reliance on port of entry controls, hold far greater promise for supporting trade while safeguarding public safety and security interests.

Outlining an ambitious vision of an integrated North American economic space, the chapter by Gary Hufbauer and Gustavo Vega-Cánovas emphasizes that the terrorist threat has added a new dimension to the NAFTA project. If economic borders have largely been dismantled under the banner of free trade, security borders have suddenly become more sensitive. Unless NAFTA comes to grips with this new reality, they argue, the progress toward closer economic integration that has been achieved could come to a halt. Under a worse-case scenario, they warn that new security barriers could prove every bit as daunting to trade and investment flows as the tariffs and quotas that were negotiated away under NAFTA. They advise that the three North American countries adopt a common project with the goal of securing North American borders while keeping them open. This common project, which Hufbauer and Vega-Cánovas call a "Common Frontier," should be sufficiently ambitious to evoke visionary leadership, but sufficiently flexible to accommodate the political realities of North America. This means that the Common Frontier should be a work in progress for at least a decade to foster the closer integration of North America while preserving the essential sovereignty of each partner.

Thomas Biersteker concludes the book by discussing the changing operational meaning of the borders that divide the United States from Canada and Mexico following the attacks of September 11. Drawing on the empirical and analytical insights of the previous chapters, Biersteker presents a synthetic summary of the book's findings, and emphasizes that the concept of the boundary needs to be decoupled from the idea of a sharp demarcation between territories. This is a point that is particularly relevant in analyzing the terrorist strikes on September 11, given that the most important "border" control failures, in this case, were actually in the consulate offices overseas that issued visas to the hijackers and the poorly secured door between the passenger cabin and the cockpit of each of the hijacked airplanes.

Final Thoughts

At first glance, the post–9-11 "war on terrorism" appears to perpetuate a decades-old cyclical pattern in which the pendulum of policy priorities swings back and forth between security and economic concerns. At the height of the Cold War in the 1960s, security issues reigned supreme. In the 1970s, economic matters overshadowed security, with "interdependence" the favorite buzzword of the decade. In the 1980s, geopolitical tensions sharpened, giving security primacy once again. In the post–Cold War 1990s, the threat of large-scale interstate warfare declined and "globalization" became the popular theme. Now, in the first decade of the twenty-first century, it seems that security is back with a vengeance. Yet this time, the primary security threat is not the traditional concern of interstate military conflict, but rather terrorism, a distinct form of organized violence orchestrated primarily by nonstate actors. Thus, borders are being fortified not against state-sponsored military invaders, but against transnational law evaders.

The awkward policy dilemma is that these clandestine actors use the same cross-border transportation and communications networks that are the arteries of a highly integrated and interdependent economy. Squeezing these arteries to filter out the bad from the good can have profound economic repercussions. And nowhere is this more evident than in North America, where the imperatives of security and of economic integration appear to be on a collision course. While this collision cannot be fully averted, how it is cushioned and managed will significantly determine the future of North American integration and cross-border relations. As the chapters in this book suggest, this means that the traditionally divorced debates about economic integration, on the one hand, and security, on the other, must now be fully joined.

Notes

1. I thank Thomas Biersteker and Veronica Kitchen for their comments. An earlier version of this chapter was presented at seminars and workshops sponsored by the Instituto Tecnológico Autónomo de México, New Mexico State University, the Université du Québec à Montréal, Dartmouth College, Queens University, the University of California at Berkeley, and Harvard University.

2. For years, the *Wall Street Journal* editorial page has advocated a constitutional amendment calling for open borders.
3. This term was popularized by the business consultant Kenichi Ohmae in *The Borderless World: Power and Strategy in an International Economy* (New York: Harper Business, 1990). After 9-11, Rosabeth Moss Kanter from the Harvard Business School commented that recent years have been "a time of tearing down walls, literally and figuratively. Now I fear we are reconstructing them." Quoted in *Boston Globe*, October 3, 2001.
4. U.S.-Mexico trade has more than tripled, and U.S.-Canada trade has nearly doubled during the past decade.
5. For example, Rep. Tom Tancredo (R-CO), chairman of the House Immigration Reform Caucus, has emphasized that defense of the country "begins with the defense of our borders." Similarly, Sen. Maria Cantwell (D-WA) says, "The fundamental question" is "how are we going to ensure the security of our borders?" See *San Antonio Express News*, September 19, 2001.
6. Lamar Smith, a member of the House Judiciary Subcommittee on Immigration has commented, "I don't think we are going to hear so much talk about open borders. We are going to be far more interested in realistic and practical solutions than in theoretical and utopian views." U.S. land borders, he says, "are too porous and offer an open invitation to those who want to harm us." Quoted in *San Antonio Express News*, September 19, 2001. Within hours of the 9-11 attacks, Dan Stein, the president of the Federation for American Immigration Reform (FAIR), stated: "The nation's defense against terrorism has been seriously eroded by the efforts of open-borders advocates, and the innocent victims of today's terrorist attacks have paid the price." Quoted in the *New York Times*, September 18, 2001.
7. *Agencia EFE*, September 30, 2001.
8. Many of the contributors first presented their ideas on February 5, 2002 at the Watson Institute for International Studies, Brown University.
9. See Peter Andreas, *Border Games: Policing the U.S.-Mexico Divide* (Ithaca, N.Y.: Cornell University Press, 2000).
10. Ibid.
11. Karl Eschbach et al., "Death at the Border," *International Migration Review* 33, no. 2 (1999): 430–54.
12. *Migration News*, September 2002.
13. *San Diego Union Tribune*, October 3, 2002.
14. See Peter Andreas and Richard Price, "From War-fighting to Crime-fighting: Transforming the American National Security State," *International Studies Review* 3, no. 3 (Fall 2001): 31–52.
15. For a detailed analysis of cross-border crime, see Ruth Jamieson, Nigel South, and Ian Taylor, "Economic Liberalization and Cross-Border Crime: The North American Free Trade Area and Canada's Border with the U.S.A." (Pts. 1 and 2), *International Journal of the Sociology of Law* (1998): 26, 245–272; 285–319.
16. The U.S. Ambassador to Canada, Paul Celluci, describes the border as "Main Street North America." Quoted in Veronica Kitchen,

"Canadian-American Border Security After September 11," unpublished paper, Department of Political Science, Brown University, May 13, 2002, 4.

17. See, for example, the *60 Minutes* segment, "North of the Border," broadcast on April 28, 2002, about terrorism and Canada's immigration and refugee system.

18. Aristide Zolberg, "Guarding the Gates in a World on the Move," Social Science Research Council, 2001, www.ssrc.orgsept11/essays/zolberg_text_only.htm.

19. *Migration News,* November 1, 2001.

20. Quoted in *Portland Press Herald* (Maine), October 4, 2001.

21. Government Accounting Office, *Customs and INS: Information on Inspection, Infrastructure, Traffic Flow, and Secondary Matters at the Detroit Port of Entry,* Washington D.C., April 22, 2002, 1.

22. See Flynn, this book, and Flynn, "America the Vulnerable," *Foreign Affairs* (January–February, 2002).

23. A truck crosses the border every 2.5 seconds—adding up to 45,000 trucks a day. See *Statement of Principles—Coalition for Secure and Trade-Efficient Borders,* wysiwyg://34/http://www.the-alliance.org/coalition/English/home.html.

24. *Financial Times,* September 17, 2001; *Globe and Mail,* March 16, 2001.

25. *Getting Back to Business: Sixth Report of the Standing Committee on Industry, Science, and Technology,* November 2001, 14.

26. Miguel Conchas, president of the Laredo Chamber of Congress, commented: "If you're going to delay everybody crossing even by one minute, that, multiplied by thousands is a nightmare...." Quoted in *St. Louis Post Dispatch,* September 29, 2001.

27. "The U.S.-Canada Smart Border Declaration," Department of Foreign Affairs and International Trade, December 12, 2001.

28. I first heard the elephant and mouse analogy to describe U.S.-Mexico relations from Joseph Lapid. Canadian Prime Minister Pierre Elliot Trudeau once described Canada's relations with the United States as the equivalent of sleeping with an elephant. In March 1969, he said of the United States, "Living next to you is in some ways like sleeping with an elephant. No matter how friendly and even-tempered is the beast, if I can call it that, one is affected by every twitch and grunt." This comment would seem to be even more relevant today.

29. Public Policy Forum, *Canada's Policy Choices: Managing Our Border with the United States,* 23.

30. This does not suggest that there is no room to maneuver or that policy choices are simply imposed. Frank Pfetsch and Alice Landau, for example, argue that negotiations in a context of structural asymmetry nevertheless often produce mutually satisfying and beneficial outcomes. See Frank Pfetsch and Alice Landau, "Symmetry and Asymmetry in International Negotiation," *International Organization* 5 (2000): 21–42. Robert Keohane and Joseph Nye point out that Canada historically has done better in negotiations with the U.S. than one might expect. See Robert Keohane and Joseph Nye, *Power and Interdependence* (Boston:

Scott, Foresman, 1989). For an insightful discussion of Canadian leverage in negotiations with the United States, see Kitchen, "Canadian-American Border Security," 16–21.

31. *The News* (Mexico City), October 2, 2001, *San Diego Union Tribune*, October 7, 2001.

32. Mexico is a popular transit point for illegal entry into the United States, which has included the smuggling of Middle East nationals. For example, prosecution documents at a federal trial in El Paso in October 2001 revealed that one smuggling group had brought in 1,000 Middle Easterners across the border since 1980. *New York Times*, October 26, 2001.

33. Adolfo Aguilar Zinser, quoted in *San Diego Union Tribune*, October 7, 2001.

34. The key piece of Canadian legislation related to 9-11 is the Anti-Terrorism Act (Bill C-36). It came into force on December 24, 2001. It amends the criminal code, the Official Secrets Act, the Proceeds of Crime (Money Laundering Act) and others. It includes measures to "deter, disable, identify, prosecute, convict and punish terrorists." See "Anti-Terrorism Act Receives Royal Assent" at www.canada.justice.gc.ca/en/news/nr/2001/doc_28215.html.

35. The 2001 budget (tabled December 10, 2001) included Can. $7.7 billion (U.S. $4.8 billion) over the next five years for "enhancing security." It includes investment in the military, air security, and border initiatives. The relevant details are in ch. 5 of the budget, www.can-am.gc.ca/pdf/bksece.pdf.

36. *Towards a Secure and Trade-Efficient Border,* Report of the Standing Committee on Foreign Affairs and International Trade and the Subcommittee on International Trade, Trade Disputes and Investment, Ottawa, November 2001.

37. See "Canada's Actions Against Terrorism Since September 11: Backgrounder," Canadian Department of Foreign Affairs and International Trade (updated May 2002), www.dfait-maeci.gc.ca/anti-terrorism/canadaactions-en.asp.

38. See chapters in this book by Clarkson, Pauly, and Hristoulas.

39. Quoted in *Toronto Sun*, September 20, 2001.

40. For an analysis of why Canada has so far shied away from embracing a formal, broadly institutionalized "security perimeter" as a solution, see Kitchen, "Canadian-American Border Security."

41. Represented, for example, by the Coalition for Secure and Trade-Efficient Borders.

42. As one scholar from Canada puts it, "Frontier or border issues have become the core of the main game of Canada-U.S. relations." Presentation by Andrew F. Cooper at conference on "Homeland Security," Dartmouth College, Hanover, N.H., May 23–24, 2002.

43. For a more detailed overview, see Malcolm Anderson, "The Transformation of Border Controls: A European Precedent?" in Peter Andreas and Timothy Snyder (eds.), *The Wall Around the West: State*

Borders and Immigration Controls in North America and Europe (Lanham, Md.: Rowman and Littlefield, 2000).

44. *Associated Press,* May 7, 2002.

45. For an argument on why we should opt for this type of approach to continental security, see the chapter in this book by Hufbauer and Vega. Before 9-11, Robert Pastor also outlined a grand vision for North America, which would even include a common currency called the "Amero." See Robert Pastor, *Toward a North American Community* (Washington D.C.: Institute for International Economics, 2001).

46. On the contrasting Mexican and Canadian approaches, see the chapter by Athanasios Hristoulas in this book.

47. For a discussion of some of these innovations, see Stephen Flynn's chapter in this book. While many of the "smart border" initiatives predate 9-11, these have been accelerated and have gained greater political support in the new security context.

48. As one Canadian official noted, "We've heard from the Mexicans that they would like to talk about a North American perimeter. Frankly, that's not in the cards right now. The government wants to focus its attention on the 49th parallel ..." He further noted that "Ms. Atkinson [from the Canadian Department of Citizenship and Immigration] was in Washington yesterday meeting with her American and Mexican colleagues, but we don't really see this as a trilateral issue at this time." Testimony of John Allen, director general, North American Bureau, before the Canadian Parliament (FAIT Committee), November 20, 2001.

2

TRADING PLACES

Canada, Mexico, and North American Security[1]

ATHANASIOS HRISTOULAS

Canadian and Mexican foreign security policy traditions can be characterized as being essentially polar opposites. Canada has always looked to multilateral and bilateral institutions for its security requirements while Mexico has preferred a more autonomous or independent course of action. And while Canada has almost always characterized its bilateral relationship with the United States as being positive-sum, Mexican decision makers have emphasized on many occasions the historically conflictual relationship between the two countries.

The aftermath of the terrorist attacks on the United States has marked an important turning point in this regard. Given their geographic proximity as well as their economic dependence on the United States, Canada and Mexico find themselves in a situation in which they must adapt to the post–9-11 security needs of their much more powerful economic partner. Indeed, leaders in all three countries recognize that changes must be made in the way goods, services, and people cross their shared borders. Yet they disagree on what kind of changes are necessary to establish and maintain North American border and continental security.

Oddly enough, the points of contention are not over what seasoned observers of the three countries' foreign policies would probably deem crucial, namely Mexico's historical unwillingness to actively participate in security institutions. In a somewhat ironic twist of fate, Mexico seems to have adopted Canada's internationalism, pushing very strongly for a multilateral approach to continental security while Canadian decision makers—consistent with past practices in the region—have conceptualized North American security as essentially a bilateral Canada-U.S. phenomenon. In that sense, a detailed examination of the position of these two states seems warranted due to their contradictory reactions to the call for North American continental and border security.

First, the chapter outlines in historical terms the nature of Canadian and Mexican foreign policy. Special emphasis is placed on demonstrating how Canada has looked to multilateral and bilateral institutions for its security requirements while Mexico has preferred a more autonomous approach. This sets the stage for the second part of the chapter, which examines the different ways continental defense has been conceived. Third, the chapter presents the specific interests of Canada and Mexico in wanting (or not wanting) a multilateral solution to continental security problems. I argue that one of the central reasons for Canada's unwillingness to pursue a multilateral solution is the result of Mexico's inclusion in the security mechanisms being discussed, while Mexico's support can be linked to the desires of President Vicente Fox's administration to turn the North American Free Trade Agreement (NAFTA) into something more than a trade arrangement.

Contrasting Foreign Security Policies: Canada and Mexico

Historically, the single most important idea in making Canadian foreign policy has been internationalism and the main goals of such a foreign policy are the avoidance of interstate war and instability in the international system.[2] To achieve these related goals, an internationalist state seeks political, social, and economic engagement of other actors in the international system because only through constructive dialogue can problems between states be resolved. Beyond the emphasis on cooperation, states with internationalist foreign policies like Canada believe that peace and stability are indivisible. In other words, "internationalists hold that the fate of any one state and the peace of the international system as a whole are interconnected."[3]

More specifically, three interrelated factors define an internationalist state: 1) A belief that each state in the international system has a responsibility for playing a constructive part in the management of conflict. 2) Multilateralism is seen as critical for defusing the clash of interests that can lead to war. 3) A strong commitment to international institutions is necessary because institutions promote multilateralism. Institutions are emphasized also because they promote rules and norms of interaction between states.[4]

Canada's internationalist orientation during the Cold War meant that the country participated actively in multilateral security institutions. For example, with particular reference to NATO, by 1952 Canada had deployed some 10,000 troops in Germany and France (including twelve air squadrons) to help defend against possible Soviet aggression. In the early years of the Cold War, Canada's NATO contingent accounted for approximately 45 percent of the Canadian defense budget. Financial constraints diminished Canada's military role in Europe in the 1970s, and with the end of the Cold War, Canada's commitment to the alliance dropped dramatically. However, Canada continued to participate actively in United Nations and NATO peacekeeping operations in the Balkans throughout the 1990s.

Along similar lines, there is a strong tradition of bilateral cooperation between Canada and the United States in matters of continental security. Beginning with World War II, Canada and the United States worked together to assure the defense of North America. In 1940, for example, Prime Minister Mackenzie King and President Franklin D. Roosevelt signed the Ogdensburg Agreement, which, through the Permanent Joint Board of Defense, institutionalized security cooperation in the event of an attack against the North American continent. The board still exists today and serves as a forum for the discussion of important military issues to Canada and the United States. Another institutionalized forum is the U.S.-Canadian Military Cooperation Committee formed in 1946. The committee manages cooperation at the military planning level. Indeed, "more than 2500 agreements to strengthen joint defense between Canada and the United States have been signed, many of which benefit Canada more than the United States in the sense that they provide access to intelligence, specialized training grounds, and finally, equipment testing facilities."[5] The most important bilateral defense treaty between the United States and Canada is the North American Aerospace Defense Command (NORAD). Created in 1957, the NORAD Center is located in Colorado and is jointly manned by U.S. and Canadian forces. The center provides early warning of missile and air attack. More important, NORAD is responsible for providing air defense in the event of an attack.

With the end of the Cold War, Canadian internationalism shifted emphasis away from the management of interstate conflict to other types of threats to international security.[6] Yet it is important to note that multilateralism is still considered a central pillar of Canadian foreign policy. In this regard, Canada continues to actively support, participate, and contribute to a wide range of multilateral international institutions.

Mexican foreign policy has gone through dramatic changes in the last decade. Historically emphasizing its independence in foreign security policy, Mexico is beginning to show signs of a greater willingness to collaborate with its neighbors to achieve regional security and stability. In particular, Mexican decision makers now realize that they can no longer isolate their country from multilateral (and bilateral) security institutions. Having much to do with the global nature of international problems, an almost stubborn defense of autonomy and independence seems to be giving way to a willingness to participate and cooperate with other states more substantially.

Legally speaking, Mexico's foreign policy is based on the constitutional principles of self-determination, nonintervention, and the peaceful solution of conflict.[7] These legal requirements have manifested themselves as foreign policy that historically can be characterized as nearly opposite to that of Canada—namely a foreign policy that emphasizes independence in foreign policymaking, especially with respect to security matters. Of particular importance here has been the distinct impact of U.S.-Mexico bilateral relations. A long-standing suspicion of U.S. motives, dating back to the war of 1846–48, further solidified Mexico's Cold War national conceptions of autonomy, independence, and nonintervention. As argued by one Mexican scholar, "the direct vicinity with such a colossus has cost Mexico ... the loss of more than half of its original territory, several military interventions, constant interference in internal political affairs and economic penetration at all levels. . . . In few countries, as is the case in Mexico, has the phenomenon of geographical situation operated as a major factor in foreign policy."[8]

The Cold War experience emphasized the need to avoid Superpower politics, and this led to a somewhat unsuccessful attempt to maintain the foreign policy orientation of nonalignment.[9] In the case of Mexico, nonalignment did not imply a complete withdrawal from international relations. On the contrary, Mexico attempted to balance the influence of superpower politics in general, and U.S. influence in particular, by taking a more active and independent role in international relations. Examples included attempts to establish solidarity with Arab and other Third World nations by openly supporting many of their causes.

Similarly, President José Lopez Portillo supported the Sandinistas in Nicaragua by withdrawing in 1979 diplomatic recognition from the Somoza regime. In 1980, after the Sandinistas had succeeded in overthrowing Somoza's dictatorship, Mexico began shipping petroleum on preferential terms to Nicaragua. Perhaps the most blatant attempt at distancing Mexican foreign policy from that of the United States was the recognition of El Salvador's rebel group—the Farabundo Martí Front for National Liberation (FMLN)—as a "legitimate political force." Similarly, in February of 1982, Portillo unilaterally issued a plan to negotiate an end to the conflict in Central America, whereby Mexico would serve as a bridge between the different parties involved in the ongoing conflict. "The then Reagan administration dismissed the Mexican initiative with annoyance and contempt."[10]

For Mexico, the first multilateral security organization in the hemisphere, the Inter-American Treaty of Reciprocal Assistance (ITRA), proved to be a nonstarter. Originally assumed by most Latin American governments to serve as a hemispheric collective security arrangement against external aggression, the "alliance" quickly expanded its role to include threats originating inside of states such as communism.[11] With this emerging reality, according to Blanca Torres, the Mexican delegation sent to Rio to negotiate the multilateral security treaty was interested primarily in minimizing the military commitments and organizational capacity of the ITRA to limit the United States' capacity to project influence and interfere in the domestic affairs of Latin American countries.[12]

Yet another regional institution—the Organization of American States (OAS)—was supported wholeheartedly by Mexico in its early years. Its government believed that the new institution might have a chance of balancing the influence of the United States within the context of hemispheric-only issues. Because the U.S. had only one vote (and no veto power), this vision did not seem all that unrealistic in 1948. However, the same events that led Mexico to attempt to undermine the goals of the ITRA also suggested that the utility of the OAS as an instrument of Mexican foreign policy was minimal. As noted by Torres, starting in 1954 with the intervention in Guatemala, Mexico began to argue that the organization had been converted into an instrument of American intervention in countries where political reform was perceived as a communist threat against U.S. national security.[13] Given this scenario, Mexico realized its purpose within the OAS was to maintain an essentially "defensive" posture against the potential for intervention. This defensive posture against the OAS turned into outright hostility when Cuba was expelled from the organization in 1958. From then on, and for the remainder of the Cold War, Mexico was extremely critical of the OAS's intended purpose. Thus, a common theme emerged in Mexican foreign policy concerning participation in multilateral security mechanisms after World War II: Such forums as the OAS and the Rio Pact—where Mexico's influence (or relative power) was insufficient to guarantee an important voice—were systematically ignored.

Recent developments suggest that Mexican foreign policy is in a transition phase, which will eventually result in a participatory foreign policy in areas where the U.S. is directly involved as well. As Ana Covarrubias argues, Mexican decision makers seem to have abandoned strict definitions of defense of sovereignty and nationalism in favor of a policy that emphasizes "pragmatism" and recognizes the limits of Mexican foreign policy.[14]

Mexico suffered dramatic economic crises in 1982, 1988, and 1994. The successive economic crises resulted in a slow but definite evolution in how Mexican foreign policy decision makers perceived the United States. These events highlighted the fact that autonomy in foreign policy and economic growth may not necessarily be compatible goals.[15] The apex of this radical reorientation regarding perceptions of the U.S. occurred in the early 1990s when Mexico, Canada, and the United States entered into negotiations to sign the North American Free Trade Agreement. Blanca Heredia argues that the signing of the NAFTA signaled three fundamental changes in Mexican foreign policy: a new openness toward the United States; a dominance of economic themes in foreign policy; and a strategic reorientation toward participation in multilateral institutions.[16]

Historically, Mexican ambivalence about multilateral institutions resulted from less than friendly U.S.-Mexican bilateral relations. This shift in the nature of U.S.-Mexican relations suggests in turn that Mexico might play a participatory role in multilateral security institutions in the future. The strongest sign of change has occurred since the terrorist attacks on the United States in September 2001. It is with this event—and the negotiations now taking place to "securitize" North America—that Mexico appears to have wholeheartedly accepted and even encouraged a multilateral security mechanism between the three NAFTA partners.

Continental Security after September 11

Continental and border security means different things to different analysts and policymakers. It runs the gamut of exchange of information and intelligence to the harmonization of immigration policy all the way to (possible) complete integration of military and public security policy and forces. The U.S. position in this debate remains unclear for the time being, yet there appears to be a general consensus that there can be no real U.S. security without cooperation with Canada and Mexico. At present, there is some security cooperation with Canada (NORAD, for example), but very little with Mexico.

The U.S. media has portrayed Canada as a hotbed for terrorist activity. Special emphasis has been placed on Canada's refugee laws, which purportedly allow terrorists to operate within the country with relative ease. As many as 300,000 immigrants and refugees enter Canada every year, and unlike other industrialized countries, Canada does not detain refugee claimants until their status can be determined. Under

Canadian law, refugees are allowed to move freely until their court appearance and as many as 10,000 individuals have not showed up for their hearings in recent years. U.S. officials and especially the U.S. media have criticized these policies as allowing terrorists and terrorist organizations to operate within the country with few restrictions. Ward Elcock, the director of the Canadian Security and Intelligence Service (CSIS) recognized this in a report submitted to Parliament when he argued, "the related policies concerning refugees and immigrants make (Canada) particularly vulnerable to terrorist influence and activities."[17]

Canadian officials are quick to respond that none of the 9-11 terrorists entered the United States from Canada. More important, Canada received approximately 37,000 refugees in 2001, 13,000 of whom requested entry to the country from U.S. territory.[18] Clearly problems exist, but the U.S. is not without blame here. For Canada, the issue is not so much the existence of terrorists in Canadian territory, but rather the somewhat ill-begotten U.S. perception that Canada might somehow represent a terrorist threat.

Second and probably more important, Canada has been slow in dealing with known terrorist groups operating within the country. The case of Ahmed Ressam, the so-called millennium bomber captured by U.S. customs and immigration officials while trying to cross the U.S.-Canada border with a trunk-load of explosives, has served as the rallying point of criticisms against the country. Ressam, an Algerian, lived in Montreal for five years as a political refugee even though a Canadian judge had ordered his deportation from the country because he had falsified travel documentation. Yet he was able to move around the country freely because the country's law enforcement agencies admit that they simply do not have the resources to track down individuals who have been ordered deported.[19]

It is this area where concerns of U.S. officials seem most warranted because, unlike refugee law—which most Canadians would vehemently defend even in light of 9-11—the underfunding of security agencies is to blame. Elcock states in his report, "With perhaps the singular exception of the United States, there are more international terrorist groups active (in Canada) than any other country in the world" and that the Counterterrorism Branch of CSIS was investigating the existence of over 50 terrorist organizations and 350 individuals for links to terrorist groups. Among the most active groups, Elcock listed Hezbollah, Hamas, the Provisional IRA, the Tamil Tigers, and the Kurdistan Workers' Party (PKK). None of these groups directly target Canadian interests, rather they use Canada as a "venue of opportunity" to support, plan, or mount attacks elsewhere."[20]

Alternatively, the U.S. concern about Mexico is that it might become a terrorist risk in the future.[21] Mexico does not have a large Muslim community where Islamic terrorists can easily "blend in" as is in the case of Canada. Yet there is fear that Al Qaeda and other terrorist organizations might somehow take advantage of the chronic weakness characteristic of many of the country's security institutions.

On a political level, President George W. Bush has ordered the various relevant government departments to begin negotiations with Canada and Mexico to ensure increased compatibility in immigration, customs, and visa policies. What this actually means in operational terms has yet to be fully developed. In that sense, according to the Conference Board of Canada, continental and border security can imply, some or all of these three elements.[22]

The first entails enhancing border efficiency by exploiting more intelligent methods to process border examinations. Here, modern technology is used to electronically or otherwise "pre-seal" a cargo vehicle at its fixed point of departure (or at designated nonborder, preclearance locations throughout the continent, which would then be easily tracked using transponders and could pass without inspection at designated border crossings). Similarly, people who work across the border and other frequent travelers could receive tamper-proof passes that would significantly ease border transit. This most basic form of continental security would turn the frontiers between Canada and the United States and Mexico and the United States into "smart" borders.[23]

The second element involves rethinking how borders are conceived. Here, Canada, Mexico, and the United States law enforcement agencies would work more closely together away from the physical frontiers to reduce the need for inspection at the borders themselves. The Conference Board refers to this strategy as moving away from the

Maginot Line of defense mentality, which tends to be static, to a defense in-depth philosophy, whereby coordination and intelligence exchange would attempt to resolve potential problems before they reach border areas.[24]

A third potential scenario involves the harmonization of immigration and refugee policy, customs clearance, and even national and public security policy to remove border inspections altogether. In this Fortress North America scenario, Canada and Mexico would forgo their own customs and immigration authorities in favor of some kind of continental authority. "Fortress North America would also include common visa requirements. In other words, both Canada and Mexico would have to adapt their relevant laws to accommodate U.S. immigration and security requirements."[25]

It is not surprising that American policymakers are pushing for some kind of continental defense scheme. On one level, the fear that terrorism lurks in Canada and possibly Mexico would be somewhat alleviated. Once in place, the United States could conceivably shift its attention and resources to other parts of the globe. Continental defense, at least from the perspective of U.S. decision makers, is a way to spread the cost of maintaining North America free of terrorism. As the U.S. begins to implement its new homeland defense policy, it seems clear that Canada and Mexico will be asked to make the necessary changes to guarantee U.S. national security. Looking at American priorities for the foreseeable future (security as opposed to trade), it is unlikely to expect otherwise. The status quo, in other words, simply is not an option. That much is not surprising.

What is surprising is how Canada and Mexico have reacted to the U.S. calls for continental security. Given the discussion above, we would expect Canada much more than Mexico to be willing to participate in some kind of common security policy. The opposite appears to be the case. While Mexico has signaled a desire to actively participate in some kind of trilateral defense mechanism with both the United States and Canada, the Canadian government has adopted an extremely cautious approach, emphasizing the need to further examine the U.S. proposal because first, it is an overly "simplistic solution" and second, it will adversely affect Canadian sovereignty.

The Canadian Position:
Sovereignty in Security Policy?

This is not to say that Canada has failed to contribute to the war against terrorism. Beyond direct military participation in Afghanistan, Canada has taken steps to change its immigration and refugee policies. Bill C-11, for example, intends to limit access to appeals by rejected refugee claimants and at the same time make it easier to deport individuals whose specific requests for asylum have been rejected. With respect especially to terrorist activities, the government introduced Bill C-36, which provides for additional resources and police powers to identify and punish terrorists and terrorist support groups. Moreover, the bill makes it illegal to raise funds on behalf of terrorists, allows the government to seize assets of terrorist organizations, and expands the police authority to pursue suspected terrorists.[26] Similarly, on an operational level, Canada-U.S. border and defense cooperation has been unprecedented in coordinating and working with intelligence and police agencies. For example, U.S. customs and immigrations officials operate in various Canadian ports and the number of F.B.I. agents operating in Canada has tripled since 9-11. Moreover, Canadian and U.S. officials are currently discussing ways to further coordinate in the areas of customs, immigration, and refugee policy. Further, the Canadian government has earmarked about U.S. $5 billion toward enhanced security, which includes, but is not limited to, intelligence and policing, emergency preparedness, military deployment, air security, and border infrastructure.[27] Finally, Canada and the United States signed the Manley-Ridge border security agreement in late 2001, when both states promised to develop further bilateral mechanisms with regards to border infrastructure. The agreement also placed special emphasis on the twin principles of coordination and information sharing as critical components of a secure common border.[28]

Security and border cooperation make good economic sense for Canada. Early in the debate over perimeter security (immediately following the terrorist attacks of September 11), Canadian officials highlighted this fact clearly by stating that "Canada must be inside any such (security perimeter) because 87 percent of our exports (go to the

U.S.)."[29] In other words, a policy where the United States inspects nearly each vehicle entering the United States from Canada would be absolutely devastating to the Canadian economy. Echoing similar concerns, the Conference Board of Canada argues that "with over 1.3 billion dollars worth of goods crossing the Canada-U.S. border every day the efficient flow of goods and people between Canada and the United States is vital to (the Canadian) economy."[30] Yet within weeks of the terrorist attacks, Canadian officials were arguing against a common continental defense. John Manley, after announcing how important it was for Canada to be inside the perimeter, later "expressed reservations telling a parliament committee that the notion that somehow or other (Canada) can solve a perceived problem by something called a perimeter is just rather simplistic . . ."[31]

One possible (and official) explanation for this policy change concerns Canadian sovereignty.[32] For example, after Paul Cellucci, the U.S. Ambassador to Canada, suggested that given economic interdependence, "perimeter" security between Canada and the United States was a "no-brainer," Canadian Prime Minister Jean Chrétien responded by stating that security was important, "but not at the expense of the people of the country."[33] The Chrétien administration argued that perimeter security would adversely affect the right of self-determination for Canadians and their elected officials, and therefore could not be considered a viable option for Canada and its citizens. In particular, Chrétien has highlighted that under perimeter security, Canada would have to modify its laws concerning immigration and refugees, something that he does not consider acceptable. More recent, in reference to Northcom and whether or not Canada would participate, Chrétien emphasized that the "defense of Canada will be assured by the Canadian government and not by the American government."[34]

Yet, oddly enough, sovereignty does not appear to be an issue for Canadian voters. In a poll conducted on October 15, 2001, by Ipsos-Reid, 70 percent of Canadians supported jointly manned border posts, 85 percent believed that Canada should make the changes that are necessary to create a joint North America security perimeter, and 81 percent said that the two countries should adopt common entry controls in treating refugees and immigrants. The same poll found that

53 percent of Canadians supported the creation of a Canadian-U.S. security perimeter, even if it meant accepting American security and immigration policies.[35] More recent surveys undoubtedly would find that Canadians are less likely to support a Canada-U.S. "security perimeter." However, this initial poll does highlight that Canadians are less sensitive about sovereignty than the country's leaders. Indeed, various provincial governments (Ontario and especially British Columbia, for example) and the wider Canadian business community have strongly supported the idea of shared continental and border security. Thus sovereignty, at least at first glance, does not appear to be a central concern for many segments of Canadian public opinion.

Beyond the sovereignty issue, the participation of Mexico in a continental security mechanism seems to pose problems for Canadian decision makers. In a parliamentary question period, Bloc Quebecois Member of Parliament Stephane Bergeron said, "What seems to bother the (former Canadian Minister of Foreign Affairs John Manley) about the idea of a security perimeter is that the discussions would involve Mexico."[36] Bergeron then argued, "Canada has everything to gain in seeing the discussions go from bilateral to multilateral. How can Canada claim to be a partner of Mexico and the U.S. in NAFTA and in the same breath exclude one of its partners from crucial discussions concerning security and trade in North America?"[37]

In response, Manley stated that Canada and Mexico do not share any borders. In this regard, the Canadian government seems to be emphasizing the idea that the kinds of security concerns that Canada and the U.S. face are completely different from the threats present at the Mexican-U.S. border. The issues facing Canada and the United States are essentially the efficient flow of legitimate goods and travelers within the context of heightened U.S. security concerns. Conversely, the U.S.-Mexican border is far more complex, characterized not only by a high level of trade, but also by the existence of illegal migration, drug trafficking, and on occasion, corruption. The negotiation of a trilateral security mechanism would therefore require much more time. Canada needs a deal as soon as possible and the introduction of a third actor, especially Mexico, would—from a Canadian perspective—unnecessarily delay the entire process or possibly stall it completely. Moreover, "smart border" technology at the Canada-U.S. border has been in place for a while, predating the terrorist attacks by a number of years. The same is not the case along the Mexican-U.S. border.

Related to this is the idea that any deal struck between Canada, Mexico, and the United States ultimately would be less than perfect from the Canadian perspective. Because police, customs, and immigration officials in Mexico are not well paid nor well trained, the possibility of "holes" in the southern flank of the perimeter would present a serious problem for the United States. And given the trilateral nature of border defense, these southern flank problems could migrate politically to the north. It is therefore clearly in the interests of Canada to exclude Mexico from the discussions. In the above context, it should not surprise any observer that the Manley-Ridge border security agreement was only bilateral.

Finally, Canadian decision makers probably feel that a trilateral NAFTA-plus border security agreement will dilute their so-called "special relationship" with the United States. Since September 11, Canadian decision makers and public opinion alike feel as though the Bush administration has not been sufficiently gracious toward Canada and its participation in the war on terrorism. Specific incidents include the now infamous (from a Canadian perspective) decision by Bush to not mention Canada as an ally in his first address to the nation after September 11 and the delayed condolences to Canada after Canadian troops were killed in a friendly-fire incident in Afghanistan. Within this context, Canadian decision makers probably feel that a trilateral security agreement will further detract from the historically close Canada-U.S. bilateral relationship.

Mexican Multilateralism

After some initial internal debate over Mexico's official position about the war on terrorism, the new Fox government has signaled its intention to strongly support the United States in its campaign. However, with legal, political, and capacity limitations, Mexico will not be contributing to the anti-terrorist campaign outside of its own borders. This does not mean that Mexico has not participated. In the days following the attacks, Mexico detained and interrogated dozens of people of Middle-Eastern origin. Moreover, the Fox government deployed police and military across the country to protect strategic facilities, public transportation, and border points. Similarly, inspection of visitors entering Mexico has more than doubled. In the case of airport security, for example, travelers must now pass through multiple electronic and physical checkpoints at the nation's airports. Finally, Mexico has begun to pay much more attention to its southern border with Central America, deploying military troops to assist immigration and customs officials.

Mexico and the United States also signed a parallel agreement on border security in early 2002. Although not as far reaching as the Canada-U.S. version, it represents an important advancement in the ongoing shift in Mexican foreign policy toward the United States. Cooperation between Mexican and U.S. officials is now routine in dealing with alien smuggling, drug trafficking, and other types of illicit activities. As outlined by Kent Paterson, "playing a central role in the massive and largely unpublicized expansion of joint U.S.-Mexico law enforcement initiatives is the Mexico-U.S. Plenary Group on Law Enforcement, created in 1995. Joint activities include the training of Mexican police, intelligence sharing, and forming cross-border task forces to fight money laundering and other crimes."[38]

As noted earlier, the central security concern for the United States regarding Mexico is not the country's immigration laws, but rather chronically weak security and immigration agencies. Yet the Fox administration is in the process of cleaning up these institutions. For example, recently the government investigated thirty-five regional chiefs of the Mexican customs service, and thirty-four were found to be involved in illicit activities and were dismissed. Although only a beginning, it demonstrates a willingness by the new government to deal with some of the more thorny issues in the bilateral relationship with the United States.

Mexico also has taken steps to demonstrate politically its solidarity with the United States in its campaign against terrorism. In October, Fox stated that Mexico "considers the struggle against terrorism to be part of the commitment of Mexico with Canada and the United States to build within the framework of the North American free trade agreement a shared space of development, well being and

integral security."[39] More recent, Jorge Castañeda, the ex-foreign minister, said, "Mexico would favor a continental approach to border security issues, extending a North American partnership that already
operates at a trade level."[40] Mexico's decision to support the NAFTA-
plus initiative marks an important turning point in the country's foreign
policy orientation. Surprisingly enough, Mexico's position on continental defense appears to be the opposite of that of the Canadians.
In the same speech, Castañeda signaled that the Mexican government
would prefer to take perimeter security "as far as possible, but that
depends on the Canadians and the Americans."[41]

The Mexican government sees continental and border security as
offering multiple opportunities in trade, security, migration, and even
social development. Similar to Canadian concerns, Mexico worries that
enhanced security at the border will hurt trade between the United
States and Mexico. But Mexico's interests go beyond simply trade.
Mexico's strategy has been one of linking issues or the attempt to trade
security for other types of benefits. The first such issue linkage is law
enforcement cooperation and technology transfer for efficient border
management, an area that Mexico desperately needs assistance, with or
without the existence of international terrorists. The Mexican ministry
of foreign relations sees this law enforcement cooperation and technology transfer as the first and most obvious way that the three NAFTA
partners can cooperate in areas beyond trade and commerce. In this
respect, the ministry has called for an integrated real-time surveillance mechanism that would enable the three countries to exchange
information on travelers and goods entering the North American
continent.

A second and more important issue linkage on the part of the
Mexican government directly relates to the expansion of NAFTA to
include other nontrade related issues. When the administration of
former President Carlos Salinas signed NAFTA in the early 1990s,
its members argued that the trilateral trade agreement would result in the improvement in the standard of living for all Mexicans.
Some eight years later, the Fox administration is under tremendous
domestic pressure to deliver on these promises. He has repeatedly
argued that as long as Mexico is a place where 40 percent of the

population makes less than two dollars a day, U.S. borders will never be secure. The solution is either a migration agreement in which the U.S. legally absorbs a substantial number of Mexican migrant workers or a North American social cohesion program similar to that in existence in the European Union or preferably both. Pushing this linkage idea even further, Mexican officials have even gone so far as to argue that it is in the national security interests of the United States to legalize the 3.5 million undocumented Mexican workers because it is better to know who they actually are, given the context of homeland defense.

Migration is the key to understanding Mexico's strong support for continental security. Yet in practical terms, Mexico only requires the support of the United States. First, migrants to Canada pale in comparison, totaling approximately 10,000 people. Second, a successful guest worker program between Canada and Mexico brings in an additional 8,000 Mexicans every year. Finally, due to geographic limitations, illegal Mexican migration to Canada is essentially nonexistent. Mexico's interest in a trilateral security arrangement is purely institutional: NAFTA must become something more than a trade agreement among the three countries because it did not deliver on its promise to raise the living standard of ordinary Mexicans. For Mexican decision makers, border security is North America's Coal and Steel Union. Consequently, the Mexican Chancellery viewed the signing of the bilateral Manley-Ridge agreement in late 2001 as disappointing and exclusionary.

Final Thoughts

Canada and Mexico appear to be at loggerheads about meaning and substance of continental security. Canadian decision makers believe border differences in North America demand a bilateral rather than trilateral approach to continental security. Furthermore, in operational terms, Canada already has made significant progress in assuring Washington that Canada should not be seen as a threat to U.S. homeland security in any way. As already noted, the Canadian and U.S. governments have slated significant resources to modernize infrastructure and cooperation among their respective law enforcement agencies has dramatically increased. The Canadian Parliament also has adopted new laws to deal with the more questionable aspects of Canadian immigration and refugee law. The same is not the case with Mexico. From a Canadian perspective, the inclusion of Mexico would unnecessarily complicate the entire process.

Alternatively, Mexico has argued repeatedly that continental security offers a window of opportunity to make NAFTA something more than a trade agreement. Through a process of policy linkage, the new Fox administration believes that Mexico can extract concessions from the United States, especially in the area of migration policy. Politically, the Fox administration has called for unprecedented trilateral cooperation in border security, law enforcement, as well as migration policy. Canada's support here is crucial in the NAFTA institutional context; yet to date, Mexico has not been able to convince Canada of its perspective on continental security. Canadian decision makers have responded by arguing that their country gains nothing by shifting the discussions from a bilateral to a trilateral format.

Not only do Mexican decision makers face resistance to their vision of continental security from Canada, but from the United States as well. Although Fox's and Castañeda's recent announcements were undoubtedly welcomed by Washington, Mexico's plan to link U.S. homeland security to areas of concern in the bilateral relationship does not appear to be working. State Department officials have stressed that although migration is an important issue in the bilateral relationship, it is presently unrelated to U.S. homeland security.

Thus, Fox faces a steep uphill battle in his attempt to sell his vision of NAFTA Plus. But that does not mean that there is nothing the administration can do. A first and obvious strategy would be to continue investing the necessary resources on infrastructure to demonstrate seriousness and commitment. Yet even here, President Fox faces tremendous internal pressure to not go too far, considering the political culture described above. Although Mexican foreign policy is much more pragmatic than it was in the past, certain political forces within the country—including an important segment of public opinion—still essentially view close bilateral relations with the United States with apprehension and concern.

Mexico also will need to demonstrate to Canadian decision makers why it is in their interests that the U.S.-Mexican border is secure and efficient. In other words, Mexico needs to demonstrate that Canada gains by going trilateral. To do this, Mexico could follow two courses of action. In the first, its decision makers could highlight that the three countries are trade partners and that what is good for one is generally good for the others. Similarly, Mexico should emphasize that under NAFTA bilateral trade has more than tripled and that this positive trend is not likely to continue if Mexico is somehow left out of the process.[42] Second, migration and social development are central not only to Mexico, but also to Canada in that they are essentially human security issues.[43] Mexico should highlight to Canadian decision makers that Fox's proposals are precisely in those areas for which Canadian officials have repeatedly argued Mexico should make changes, and therefore Canada should be more consistent in its foreign policy behavior, especially with an increasingly important trade partner.

Washington appears to have a minimum position regarding Canada, Mexico, and continental security. On the one hand, the United States wants Canada to toughen its rules dealing with immigrants and refugees. Yet with respect to Mexico, it desires the modernization of customs and immigration control and the elimination of corruption. As the new homeland security policy evolves, both countries will need to recognize that the actor with the greatest amount of leverage in the discussions over continental and border security is the United States. Given the dynamics of the Latino vote in the United States as well as the comparatively friendly and personable relationship between Presidents Fox and Bush, Canada will probably have to accept some kind of Mexican participation. However, Mexico might discover that the U.S. is simply too distracted to discuss continental migration and development policy for the time being.

Notes

1. The author would like to thank the Asociacion Mexicana de Cultura A.C. for its ongoing financial support and Peter Andreas and Thomas Biersteker for their helpful comments on an earlier draft of this chapter. Gaby Sosa and Nallely Aguilar provided invaluable research assistance.

2. Kim Richard Nossal, *The Politics of Canadian Foreign Policy* (Ontario: Prentice Hall, 2000).
3. Ibid., 53.
4. Taken from ibid., 54–60.
5. David Jones, "Fortress North America," *Ehgloo Magazine,* January 21, 2002, www.ehgloo.com/archive/northamerica/dj020121.htm.
6. Nossal, *Politics.*
7. Raul Benitez Manaut, "Sovereignty, Foreign Policy, and National Security in Mexico, 1821–1989," in Hal Klepak (ed.), *Natural Allies? Canadian and Mexican Perspectives on International Security* (Ontario: Carleton University and FOCAL, 1996).
8. Mario Ojeda, *Alcances y límites de la política exterior de México* (Mexico City: El Colegio de México, 1981): 87–88.
9. Peter H. Smith, *Talons of the Eagle* (Oxford,U.K.: Oxford University Press, 1996).
10. Ibid., 211.
11. Gordon Connel Smith, *The Inter-American System* (Oxford, U.K.: Oxford University, 1966).
12. Blanca Torres, *De la Guerra al mundo bipola. México y el mundo* (Mexico City: Senado de la República, 2000): 83.
13. Ibid., 83–90.
14. Ana Covarrubias, "El problema de los derechos humanos y los cambios en política exterior," *Foro Internacional* 39, no. 4, (1999): 429–452.
15. Blanca Heredia, "El dilema entre crecimiento y autonomía: reforma económica y reestructuración de la política exterior en México," in CEI-COLMEX & IMRED (eds.), *La política exterior de México. Enfoques para su análisis* (Mexico City: El Colegio de México-IMRED, 1997).
16. Ibid., 81.
17. Ward Elcock, *Submission to the Special Committee of the Senate on Security and Intelligence,* Ottawa, June 24, 1998, www.csis-scrs.gc.ca/eng/miscdocs/ kelly_e.html.
18. Allan Thompson, "Flow of Refugees at Heart of Deal," *The Toronto Star,* October 26, 2001; and "Canada Bound Asylum Seekers Housed in New York Refugee Shelter," *Associated Press,* June 27, 2002.
19. See "Canada's Importance," *Boston Globe,* October 1, 2001.
20. "Report of the Special Senate Committee on Security and Intelligence," *Senate of Canada Committee Reports,* 1999, www.parl.gc.ca/36/1/parlbus/ commbus/senate/com-e/secu-e/rep-e/repsecintjan99part1-e.htm.
21. Robert Leiken, "Enchilada Lite: A Post–9/11 Mexican Migration Agreement," in *Center for Immigration Studies,* 2002, www.cis.org/articles/2002/ leiken.html.
22. "Border choices: Balancing the Need for Trade and Security," *The Conference Board of Canada,* 2001: 3–5, www.conferenceboard.ca/ pubs/borderchoices.10.01.pdf.
23. Ibid., 3.
24. Ibid., 4.
25. Ibid., 5.

26. "Canadian Anti-terrorism Act Tabled: New Powers to Fight Terrorism," *Canada on Line*, 2001, at Canadaonline.about.com/library/weekly/ aa101701a.htm.

27. "Heading off the Terrorist Threat: Canada Takes Decisive Action," in *Canada World View: Department of Foreign Affairs and International Trade* 14, (Winter 2002): www.dfait-maeci.gc.ca/common/search/menu-en.asp.

28. "Security and Opportunity at the U.S.-Canada Border," White House Web site, June 28, 2002, www.whitehouse.gov/news/releases/2002/06/20020628.html.

29. "Securing our Future: Report of the Standing Committee on Finance," *House of Commons Committee* Reports, 2001, www.parl.gc.ca/InfoComDoc /37/1/FINA/Studies/Reports/.

30. "Border Choices" in *Conference Board*, 1.

31. Tom Cohen, "U.S. Ambassador Details 'No-brainer' Security Plan," *The Daily Camera*, October 6, 2001.

32. DeNeen L. Brown, "Canada Wary of U.S. Anti-Terror Plan: Some Fear a Continental Defense System Would Threaten Ottawa's Sovereignty," *The Washington Post*, Sunday, February 24, 2002.

33. David Dicke, "Canadian Sovereignty Called into Question in Fight against Terrorism or the U.S. is Ready to Add More States," www.davidicke.net/newsroom/america/canada/100401a.html.

34. John Ward, "New American Military Structure No Threat to Sovereignty: Chrétien," *The Canadian Press*, April 17, 2002.

35. For more information on this and other related polls, see Ipsos-Reid, www.angusreid.com/media/dsp_pre_more_cdn.cfm.

36. "Report of the Standing Committee on Foreign Affairs and International Trade," *House of Commons Committee Reports*, 2001, www.parl.gc.ca/InfoComDoc /37/1/FINA/Studies/Reports.

37. Ibid.

38. Kent Paterson, "Deepening U.S.-Mexico Security Cooperation: As NAFTA's Anti-narcotics Apparatus Focuses on Public Security, Human Rights Activists Grow Worried," *Borderlines* 84 no. 9, (December 2001): 3.

39. Ibid.

40. "Mexico Would Support Shift to Security Perimeter with U.S. and Canada," *The Canadian Press*, February 2, 2002, www.cp.org/english/hp.htm.

41. Ibid.

42. According to the Department of Foreign Affairs and International Trade (DFAIT), Mexico is Canada's largest trading partner in Latin America, and Canada has become Mexico's second-largest export market after the United States. For Canada, Mexico is its third-largest source of imports. Mexico ranks as Canada's fourth-largest export market; "Mexico Trade Relations," Department of Foreign Affairs and International Trade, (2002).

43. Human security, as defined by DFAIT, "means taking the security of ordinary people as a central point of reference, rather than simply the security of territory or governments. A human security agenda means working to ensure that people need not fear for their rights, their safety or even their lives." "Canada's Human Security Web Site," Department of Foreign Affairs and International Trade (2002), www.humansecurity.gc.ca/psh-e.asp.

3

BORDERING ON THE IMPOSSIBLE

U.S.-Mexico Security Relations after 9-11

MÓNICA SERRANO

By now 9-11 has been well and truly branded as not just a traumatic, but also a quasi-apocalyptic date, in the mythography of the American psyche. From the nemesis of Ground Zero has arisen a new spirit of determination to pursue and win a war on terrorism—a catharsis that may be delayed in coming, but that definitively derives from that zero time near the start of the American twenty-first century. An evil destruction that originated a new epic adventure of quest and crusade, the event of 9-11 fits the mythic bill of the Western past in a distinctively American manner. Even if it gives way to future apocalypses—and indeed, that it will is very much in the American nature of apocalypses—9-11 now ranks with the classic American myths of adversity and triumph, war against evil and war's holy grail, new world order.

Myths as quintessential to a nation as 9-11 are notoriously difficult for outsiders to grasp. For outsiders, these myths seem to be mere smoke screens for the sordid designs of imperial expansion and conquest. The devotees of myth expect at the least a recognition from the outside world that scores somewhere between respect and reverence for both their suffering and mission. At the same time, outsiders who either fail to understand the stakes of the demand on them, or who just cannot bring themselves to respond with a quota of empathetic generosity, are easily cast as taboo-breakers and suspect disbelievers beyond the pale. For outsiders with a history of antagonistic ambivalence about the newly regenerated mythic nation—that is to say, neighbors—the time when they ought to be generous in principle may instead bring forth what, for want of a better euphemism, one may call unkindness. Such, with some shadings, was the Mexican response to 9-11.

To put it unkindly, 9-11 may have been difficult to comprehend for the Mexican public, but it was not traumatic. Much less so was it apocalyptic. Compared to the emotional outpouring of support from Tony Blair, Mexico's response to the terrorist attacks was delayed, distanced, and clearly mishandled. The lack of public and spontaneous expressions of sympathy and swift official acts of solidarity, as well as the display of arrogant contempt by the opposition parties for the ill-phrased declarations of Mexico's foreign minister, all spoke to the depth of Mexico's alienation from the U.S. that may well seem shocking to the U.S. This certainly needs to be addressed in future considerations of the U.S.-Mexico security relationship.

Before 9-11, relations between these neighbors were often charac-terized as an uneasy marriage between unequal partners, perhaps even a marriage of inconvenience, given the inferior partner's perception of threat. Yet it was a marriage in which divorce was impossible due to the opportunities on offer. Such cozy platitudes now need to be de-stroyed, if what was at stake in 9-11 was indeed less a critical juncture in the relationship, than a semi-apocalyptic point of departure for the U.S. To ask how Mexico could have failed to understand this—how the catastrophe across the border could have elicited not closeness, but distance on the part of Mexico—is clearly of special pertinence from a security perspective. Simultaneously, the security perspective on U.S.-Mexican relations should recall, beyond the technical terminology, that we are talking about neighbors—parties who for normative and prag-matic reasons ought to cooperate on the basis of mutual understanding. Without this understanding, where is the security?

Unfortunately, what ought to be the case runs smack up against history, the old enemy of both the ideal and, as it happens, the mythic. Not only will the history of U.S.-Mexican relations not go away; much more lamentably, the bad blood between kin tends to spill out precisely when attempts are made to put their differences behind them. Rather than a mere rehearsal of old conflicts, the history of U.S.-Mexican rela-tions is one in which moves toward cooperation have been attempted, but tend only to fall apart at the old seams of sovereign distrust and incomprehension. To know why neighbors cannot get along is less a question of history (although there is a history), than one about why they are so bad at cooperating.

In this light security relations are a microcosm of a larger dynamic of failure. The terminology of security cooperation points toward the ideal principles of neighborliness, since from the idea of security regulation we soon pass to notions of security cooperation and community. Here if anywhere, we might expect the gap of the border to have been closed, for neighbors to have become close. To understand the failure of the security regulation paradigm will be a first step toward looking into the black hole of U.S.-Mexican relations exposed by 9-11.

Sources of Security Cooperation between the U.S. and Mexico from the 1950s

The inescapable reality of Mexican (as Canadian) foreign policy has been managing the bilateral relation with the U.S. and dealing with the asymmetries built into that relation. But in sharp contrast to Canada, security relations between Mexico and the U.S. from the second half of the twentieth century have been marked by both the absence of an institutional framework and a complex pattern of intermittent cooperation, withdrawal, and persistent disagreement over the meaning and content of regional and bilateral security threats.

In the course of the past century, the security dialogue between the hegemonic power and its southern neighbor was hardly played to the tune of shared strategic interests. Still, security cooperation between the two countries, however rare, occasionally reappeared when so demanded by common perceptions of serious external threats. The revealing cases are twofold. On the one hand, there was an ephemeral belief in trust and shared interests that prompted the smaller partner to bet on the outcome of a special relation. On the other hand, there were those common external threat perceptions that prompted Mexico to set aside its defensive and nonmilitaristic concept of security and accept closer military and security cooperation. In a limited number of critical junctures, such considerations led the Mexican government to forgo deeply entrenched qualms about military and nonmilitary security cooperation with its northern neighbor.[1]

There are three outstanding instances involving institutional and semiformal forms of defense and security cooperation between Mexico and the U.S. First, the negotiation of the Joint Defense Commission in 1941; second, the negotiation of a regional nonproliferation regime; and third, the steps initiated by the civilian elite in the context of the Gulf War, reinforced in turn by its acquiescence in the militarization of anti-narcotic policies. These milestones paved the way for the 1996 bilateral agreements on defense sand security cooperation and subsequently to President Fox's declaration calling for a North American Security Policy in the aftermath of the September terrorist attacks.[2]

Yet even the most cursory survey of these exceptional cases also makes it abundantly clear how, as the Mexican government moved toward closer cooperation, concerns about territorial sovereignty and national independence in fact continued to influence security negotiations. This was clearly the case of the 1941 Joint Defense Commission, modeled on the Canadian-American example. It was intended to study and develop joint defense plans along three main fronts: hemispheric defense, bilateral security relations, and the defense of California. But between 1938 and 1942, interpretations of the content, scope, and implementation of agreed issues—including access to Mexico's airspace, the use and construction of ports and radars—remained contentious.[3] Only when the context changed, first with the attacks on Pearl Harbor and then with the sinking of two Mexican ships by German forces, did differences over these and other matters finally evaporate. Even when the determination to pursue security and defense cooperation was partly a response to the perception of common security threats, practical considerations of self-interest, including the possibility of settling long-standing differences over the nationalization of oil companies, also held sway with the Mexican government.

President Cárdenas expressed willingness to collaborate with the U.S. war effort as early as 1938. In a sequence that may well have resonances today in Mexico, contacts and negotiations between military personnel of both countries began secretly, with the express aim of avoiding a nationalist backlash within Mexico. Even as such manifestations of cooperation as the training and restructuring of Mexican military personnel and territorial defense were proceeding, along with the creation of the Pacific Military Region under Cárdenas' command, all was conducted on a "softly softly" basis. The precedent was set for what in Mexican eyes may be termed "low profile cooperation"—or what to some may have appeared as backhanded cooperation. Similarly, even though Mexican border airports (just as Canadian) would play a vital role in assisting with diverted airline flights after 9-11, this was a fact that the Fox government would choose not to advertise to its public in a clear homage to this Mexican tradition. In 1942, the government of Avila Camacho had gone even further down the road of covert cooperation by petitioning for U.S. military personnel deployed in Mexican territory to be dressed in civilian clothes.[4]

The end of World War II and the subsequent advent of the Cold War brought a halt to defense cooperation between Mexico and its northern neighbor. Mexico's foreign policy reverted to its traditional principles of nonintervention and the peaceful settlement of disputes. From the U.S. perspective, the formal framework provided by a dormant Joint Defense Commission, together with the permanent presence of a military attaché and, above all, political stability south of the border, may have proved sufficient to reassure the U.S. government about the safety of its southern flank. A low profile from Mexico could not be without its advantages.

Moreover, in the context of nuclear disarmament and arms control negotiations, the nuclear monopoly of the hegemonic power was not fundamentally challenged by Mexico's disarmament policies. It could even be argued that by promoting the goal of nuclear nonproliferation in Latin America, the Mexican government contributed to the wider nuclear arms control effort. Although often interpreted as an example of foreign policy independence, a closer look at Mexico's nuclear nonproliferation policy in the aftermath of the 1962 Cuban Missile Crisis, reveals symptoms of security cooperation, albeit tacit. The prescriptions to control nuclear weapons were drawn both from genuine concerns about the danger posed by these weapons, as well as from the mutual interest of nuclear powers in keeping the stability of the central strategic balance. And, as had been the case earlier, the expectation of material and nonmaterial rewards may have also featured in Mexico's determination to pursue the negotiation of a regional nuclear-free zone.[5]

In both cases of World War II and, more arguably, of nuclear non-proliferation, Mexico and the U.S. could work together on the basis of shared perceptions of external threats. While not the whole story, such convergences of perception are clearly fundamental to shaping the "special relation" between the two countries. The problem arises when there are no common enemies to make the neighbors friends. For all the conditions set upon cooperation during World War II, Mexico was more of an ally to the U.S. than Ireland to Britain. Yet by the Central American Crisis of the 1980s, Mexico and the U.S. could hardly have pursued more divergent policies. What was needed after that hiatus was a fresh impetus toward commonality of interest. It came with NAFTA (the North American Free Trade Agreement). Unfortunately, NAFTA would also run into security complications such as those bound with the third key instance of cooperation mentioned above, the militarization of anti-narcotic policy along the border.

Economic Integration and Security Cooperation: the Bride and her Dowry

The negotiation of NAFTA involved a radical shift in Mexico's foreign policy and in the country's bilateral relationship with the United States. As its performance and evolution have rapidly exceeded most expectations, it is hard to remember that NAFTA was originally intended to remain as no more than a trade agreement. That its evolution has not conformed entirely to this blueprint, itself says much about the many ways in which wider political and security considerations have come to bear on NAFTA.

Clearly, the ever-thickening web of trade and investment now meshing together Canada, the U.S., and Mexico speaks volumes for NAFTA's economic success. The factors underlying this success are by now reasonably well established.[6] By contrast, assessments of NAFTA in political and security terms are only beginning to be made. They are likely to be controversial, but nowhere more so than in the conjunction of rapid economic integration with demands for tighter security coordination. 9-11 is a watershed here as well, but one for which a history has been building, since the foundation of mutually beneficial economic cooperation was laid.

As was the case in 1993 (during the negotiation of the free trade agreement), the efforts made at the turn of the new century by the Ministry of Foreign Affairs to "deepen" NAFTA set off a heated debate about the conduct of relations with the northern neighbor. Then as now, the underlying issue has not been whether deepening NAFTA is desirable or not, but whether there are available avenues to achieve this goal, and the potentially harmful consequences for Mexican culture and identity. For more than a decade this long debate has made clear the existence of a fundamental consensus among Mexican political elites and the public at large regarding the perceived benefits of NAFTA.[7] But such consensus has not proved strong enough to uproot old and new qualms about the northern neighbor, either within Mexico's political elite or public.

It is true that the context in which this debate has taken place has significantly changed over the years, and yet the transition to democracy has not removed disagreement about Mexico's own domestic views of international relations—especially that of bilateral relations with Washington. Indeed, in line with earlier Mexican experiences of approaching cooperation with the U.S., there is a case for saying that bilateral relations worked better when tacit—that the explicit implementation of NAFTA had the unfortunate consequence of disrupting tacit understandings with the U.S., as it both patently reduced the margin of maneuver long enjoyed by Mexico's foreign policy, and set off a depth charge in the debate of Mexico's domestic policies. What emerges is a modern instance of the classic pattern of nothing failing like cooperative success: on the one hand, widespread and genuine commitment to the trajectory of NAFTA; on the other, deep reluctance to accede too far to what is perceived as high-risk, U.S.-led agendas and pressures. It is a syndrome that Mexico's response to 9-11 bears all too eloquently stubborn testimony.

In the political realm, while the Fox administration emerged from the 2000 elections with a much higher degree of internal and external legitimation than its predecessors, it has been unable to translate such legitimacy into significant policy achievements on either front, (whether or not the long ascendancy of the Institutional

Revolutionary Party [PRI] over the legislative and executive powers is to blame for this). On the external front, foreign policy decisions, particularly the conduct of the bilateral relationship with the U.S., have emerged as the main bone of contention between the executive and the legislative power. The chain of disagreements over relations with Cuba, Mexico's adherence to the International Criminal Court, and the prerogatives of the executive on foreign policymaking all tell a similar tale of self-sabotaging uncertainty in Mexico. While the Senate's rebellion against Foreign Minister Jorge Castañeda's determination to resuscitate the "special relationship" with the U.S. and to deepen NAFTA can certainly be explained in terms of a political agenda dictated by the internal electoral calendar, party political opposition also taps into a deeper, more obdurate vein of skepticism vis-à-vis rapprochement with the U.S.

Why should skepticism persist in the teeth of cooperative success? If we are to seek rationality in the ambivalence of the Mexican posture, we might do well to look beyond the culturalist arguments about identity and look instead at security relations—or rather, to see security relations between Mexico and the U.S. as now being heavily imbued with symbolic cultural meaning. We might look at the place that joins the issue of security with that of cultural identity: the border.

The U.S.-Mexico border is a contraflow of contradiction. In one direction flows the massive tide of free trade. In the other, flows the massive securitization by Washington of drug-control and migration policies. Free trade overruns the demarcatory concept of the border; to prevent drugs and immigrants from overrunning the border, the concept of the border becomes punitively demarcatory. The border does not exist, yet the border is controled. It is not possible to explain the ambivalence in Mexico's official and public attitudes toward the U.S. without an appreciation of these objective and culturally potent contradictions. Indeed, Mexican vacillation between cooperation and skepticism looks like a mirror image of the double thought of the U.S. about its own border.

How was control of the concept of the border lost? This occurred by the terms of security cooperation agreed to under the aegis of NAFTA. In the 1990s, security cooperation between Mexico and the U.S. was resumed on the assumption that cross-border externalities—including migration flows, environmental effects, and the trade in narcotic drugs and other illicit commodities—need to be managed and contained. Yet the underlying premise on which calls for cooperation rested, and indeed still rest, was new: Namely, security cooperation would now itself be tied into the net of structural factors making for closer integration and tighter interdependence. No longer a backhander, security cooperation would now be a card in a full hand.

Drawing on the "security regulation" paradigm, security cooperation between Mexico and the U.S., post-NAFTA, has proceeded in the belief that the political will to cooperate and to act in concert is all that is needed to meet external challenges and to regulate negative spillovers from tighter economic interdependence. The conviction is that solutions will simply flow from the maximization of bilateral cooperation; the lurking assumption that all these problems are only blips to be expected from closer economic integration and denser transnational flows. Above all, the "security regulation" paradigm works on the assumption that each of the partners obtains net security benefits that outweigh the costs of securitizing.

Gradual steps toward security cooperation between Mexico and the U.S. started in the early 1990s in this landscape of assumptions. History soon made the objection that it is too easy to make with analytical hindsight—that security cooperation depends on a shared view of both the means and goals of security policy. When the views diverge, the cooperation can still continue, but in the manner of a tandem bicycle with only one free wheel. To put it another way, what distinguished security cooperation between Mexico and the U.S. from those of other partners in economic integration has been Mexico's reluctant adoption of policies and responses forcefully "promoted" by Washington. The expansion of the military's role in drug and border control, the development of mobile forces, interagency operational teams, as well as the creation of a bilateral high level contact group, are all good examples of how the process of defining security policies has taken place under duress rather than through convergence. Security cooperation has been forthcoming from Mexico, albeit sometimes in a foot-dragging way, while the question "whose security?" has been left to hang in the air. The reality, as well as the perception, of security cooperation post-NAFTA, has been that Mexican governments have had little choice but to come to terms with U.S. priorities in the face of non-traditional threats, and with U.S. responses to them, particularly drug trafficking.

Were that the end of the story, it would be bad enough. That it was going to get worse ought to have been apparent when NAFTA's impressive economic dynamism was not sufficient on its own to contain conflict over drug control and undocumented migration issues, or indeed to persuade policymakers in Washington to reverse or reconsider their securitization.[8] The security regulation paradigm that was established to help NAFTA began to look like an overrun border. Harder lines started to be drawn.

It's the Drugs, Stupid

In a desperate attempt to stop the flow of illicit drugs and migrants, from the mid-1980s the U.S. increasingly relied on unilateral repressive measures. In 1986, National Security Decision Directive NSDD 221 defined drug trafficking as a threat to U.S. national security. Undocumented migration was added. The decision was motivated both by the surge in drug consumption in the U.S. and possibly also by intelligence about the links between drug traffickers and revolutionary guerrilla organizations. Likewise, through the 1980s, the combination of "pull" and "push" factors (among which the debt crisis and civil war in Central Amercia were undoubtedly the most important) had propelled undocumented migration. The compounded effect of these trends was the perception in the U.S. of a loss of control of the border with Mexico. Suddenly, but also simultaneously with NAFTA, the imperative was to regain "control" over the border. Hence both the increasingly punitive approach of U.S. drug and migration control policies and the bureaucratic, military, and financial field days enjoyed by border enforcement agencies.

The expansion of border police agencies and "smart" surveillance technologies, symbolically encapsulated by "Operation Hard Line," was as extraordinary as it was unilateral. Between 1990 and 1998 the Immigration and Naturalization Service almost tripled, the cadres of the Border Patrol doubled, as did those of the Drug Enforcement Agency, while federal law enforcement budgets allocated to the

"Southwest" border shot from U.S. $1 billion in 1993 to approximately U.S. $1.7 billion in 1998.[9] What had been a relatively flexible and locally managed border regime was indeed progressively "hardened" as the defense of the border expanded dramatically, symbolically, and—one might say—uncontrollably in the course of a mere decade. Holding the line would involve the U.S. moving from a forward defense aimed at impeding the "entry of contraband goods or persons," to a rear "border-intensive" line of defense directed at disrupting the distribution of illicit goods and the movement of undocumented migrants.

This defensive build-up of get-tough U.S. border agencies, initiatives and budgets has all been geared by the supply control paradigm, proceeding on the assumption that the sources of the contraband problem are eminently external. Application of the paradigm would contain and dry up the flow of illicit goods and undocumented migrants by singling out the border as a "target rich opportunity zone." Crucially, it also would seek to enlist the collaboration of producing, out-migrant, and transit countries. Indeed, it was because of this perceived externality of threat that cooperation could be sought (and at times coerced) from Mexico. But this is where the sting in the tail of this accelerated history comes: having cooperated, as in the past, on the basis of a common front against an external threat, Mexico found that the U.S. line was both retreating from and turning against it. Even as trade flows between the two countries gathered force, the definition of drug trafficking and illegal migration as significant threats to national security positioned Mexico as a potential threat to the U.S. Letdowns do not get much harder than that.

As the U.S. South Florida Task Force redeployed and tightened interdiction efforts in the first half of the 1980s, Mexico had already been carved out as the main transit route for 60–70 percent of the cocaine entering the U.S. market. Confronted by this intractable problem, but also seduced by the good news of the supply control paradigm (an external threat) and swayed by the appeal of common security regulation (with a special relationship to trade in the bargain), the Zedillo government in the second half of the 1990s bit the bullet: hitherto low-profile military cooperation leaped up and out into the open in the form of U.S. military transfers and military procurement in Mexico. The military orientation given to anti-narcotics policies in the second half of the 1980s by the U.S. had finally been acceded to by Mexico. The militarization of security cooperation along the border appears to have been the price Mexico paid for the free gift of NAFTA.

Need the "order the border" policy have failed? After all, the escalation of the war on drugs did result in mounting Federal cocaine seizures from 2 tons in 1981 to 27 tons in 1986, and up to around 100 tons in 1990.[10] Likewise with the human cargo that came with the drugs, apprehensions by the U.S. Border Patrol were at 1,516,000 by the end of the 1990s, which is certainly a performance improvement on the 400,000 of the early 1970s.[11] Yet such figures are only half the story, as the extensive literature on both drug interdiction and anti-immigration policies now tells us. While the seizures were going up, so too were the U.S. import price differentials of heroin, cannabis, and cocaine, selling at seventy, fifteen and eight times their licit prices respectively in the U.S. during the 1990s. To the extent that tighter interdiction increased the total volume of exports needed to deliver a ton of cocaine, it helped stimulate the demand for drugs in the U.S. Similarly, in 1996, the estimated resident Mexico-born population in the U.S. of 4.8 million legal residents was being challenged by an influx of between 2.3 and 2.4 million undocumented migrants. From 1997 to 2002 alone, the Mexican illegal migrant population could have increased by nearly 1 million people. The precise figures may escape us, but not the conclusion that in overall numbers the 1990s were the decade of the highest immigration in the history of the U.S.[12]

If the policy failed, then whose fault is it? Mexico's—if you are the U.S.; the U.S.'s—if you are Mexico. Blame is easier to share than cooperation. From the U.S. point of view, permissiveness and relatively stable patterns of corruption in Mexico had provided fertile ground for the relocation of cocaine traffickers there in the 1980s. There is some truth in this. Nor can there be doubt that successive Mexican governments bear social responsibility for the "push" factors that prompt hundreds of thousands of citizens to migrate to the U.S. Why, we can hear the Washington policymakers asking, could not Mexico put its house in order?

"And why," we hear Mexico's answer echo to the U.S., "have your policies wreaked such havoc in our house? If it is true that widespread corruption and illicit practices provided fertile ground for the boom of drug trafficking, isn't it also the case that it was in the spheres of illegality dilated by punitive enforcement that drug trafficking came to take permanent residence with us, with the curse of transnational organized crime hot on its heels? Let us not downplay the role of restrictive and prohibitionist policies in exacerbating the drug problem! Isn't the uncontroled magnitude of drug-related corruption, violence, and social disruption suffered in Mexico throughout the 1990s to be laid at the door of Washington's determination to securitize drug control policies and to escalate the war on drugs—all a price for being one's neighbor's keeper? As for migration, let's look at 'pull' as well as push factors. Shielding your border is all very well and good, but there are such things as dynamic synergies between push and pull. Is criminalizing migration flows really the best we can do?"

The U.S. may well want to say, "What about the continuing evidence of corruption in our—let's agree—long-suffering neighbor? From the dismantling of the Dirección Federal de Seguridad in the mid-1980s, to the scandals surrounding the dissolution of the National Institute to Combat Drugs in 1997, to the hopes dashed in 2001 by revelations of transborder corruption running through the once highly praised Beta border law enforcement groups, there is a litany of illustrations of the chronic proneness of law enforcement agencies in Mexico to corruption.[13] What is the price of cooperation from a neighbor like this?"

In short, the answer to why the policy of securitizing the U.S.-Mexico border has failed depends on which side of it you are on. Impartiality is impossible. Both sides are right and wrong. This is why the problem of mutually generated threats has surfaced recurrently in bilateral tensions over the extent of Mexico's cooperation in and commitment to the war on drugs. It also accounts for mounting frustration in Mexico in the face of diminishing returns—and undesired effects—of punitive forms of undocumented migration enforcement. The hardening of the border has increasingly turned migration into a violent, profitable, and organized enterprise, while immigration amnesties in the United States have only enhanced Mexico's magnetic field as a transit point. It could be argued that U.S. policies have contributed as much as poor economic and political management to the perception of Mexico as a threat. But here we return to the sticking point and the suspension of the blame game: Though it may be a special plea about the perverse effects resulting from the unprecedented unilateral build-up of border controls, Mexico stands on the wrong side of the line. Stationed as a Trojan threat, Mexico finds many of the doors to constructive security cooperation closed. The upshot is that the contention that increased cooperation along the lines of the dominant anti-narcotics paradigm would restore order along the border and bolster Mexico's security now looks like an unkind joke played in the fast lane of history.

Of course, the U.S. has also drawn its own conclusion. The U.S. perception of Mexico as a threat and the persistent trend toward punitively sealing the border go hand in hand. Whether forward or rear, the American notion of homeland defense has now spilled symbolically onto the border. The immediate American response to the attacks of 9-11 of closing its borders follows from this experiment in securitization at the southern border. In a paradoxical reversal of its history with Mexico, the U.S. now appears to be an empire in retreat. But while this "de-invasion" may be about holding the line of the border, it also leaves behind it a new form of control: not that of territorial conquest, but that of territorial redefinition. Sharing a border with the U.S. now threatens Mexico with just such a redefinition of its sovereignly symbolic self from loyal adjunct to wild frontier.[14]

U.S.-Mexico Security Cooperation in the Aftermath of 9-11: What Chance?

It was within this thinly institutionalized and highly conflictual context of security cooperation that newly elected President Fox presented his calling card to the United States, bidding for a new special relationship to be based on a deepening of NAFTA on the model of the European Union. Foreign Minister Jorge Castañeda articulated a new principle for Mexican foreign affairs, one of "multilateralism-bilateralism"—the best of all worlds, perhaps—but one that would be anchored in recognition of "U.S. hegemony."[15] The signs were that the new, impeccably credentialed, Mexican administration of 2000 was aiming for an upgrade in Mexico's relations with the U.S., not least in terms of security cooperation in which joint operations against drug trafficking intensified. Castañeda also was aiming high in his declared ambition of gaining a profile for Mexico on the international stage, specifically through a new and activist emphasis on the protection of human rights in its foreign policy.

Reconstructing the pieces of this early combined strategy, we can appreciate its logic as well as hopefulness. Mexico would again become the friendliest of neighbors to the U.S.—and would receive in return concessions on what emerged as the cause closest to President Fox's heart, the plight of Mexican illegal immigrants in the U.S. and the dangers faced in illegal border crossings. NAFTA was to be deepened, security on the drug border to be given, promises on the immigration front to be brought back—it was all going to happen like a dream. And many must have thought indeed that they were dreaming when President Bush affirmed Mexico's top position in the U.S. foreign policy agenda, and President Fox said "thank you" by requesting an amnesty for the 3.5 million of undocumented Mexicans living in the U.S.[16]

9-11 occurred just six days after President Bush's declaration. If Mexican civil society was not left reeling, its diplomacy was. Overnight, the U.S. tore up its list of top priorities, and reverted to its border fixation. Indeed, nine months after 9-11, a much more heavily guarded border than the U.S. border with Canada has not been enough to reassure the U.S. about the southern border's safety, with transit delays there remaining two hours above the 20–minute average that preceded the attacks.[17] Clearly, here was the dilemma for the Fox-Castañeda dream team. How close would the U.S. allow its porous neighbor? Should Mexico move closer first?

A hardly coincidental combination of declarations in April 2002 sheds light on some of the choreography that must have transpired to bring the two neighbors closer than ever before. First, the Mexican Foreign Ministry issued some stinging criticisms of Cuba's human rights record, to accompany Mexico's unprecedented abstention from a vote condemning Cuba at the fifty-seventh session of the U.N. Human Rights Commission. Days later, Washington announced the imminent creation of a Northern Command (Northcom)—an organizational structure charged with ensuring the defense of the three NAFTA partners, along with parts of the Caribbean and the

contiguous waters in the Pacific and Atlantic. While Northcom institutional innovations mostly refer to the organization of U.S. forces,
it will also have responsibility for defending U.S. airspace and coasts.
In Mexico as in Canada, the government insisted that Northcom is
strictly a U.S. venture that will not involve Mexican troops, territory, or
sovereignty. However, the visit paid by Mexico's defense minister, General Gerardo Clemente Vega Garcia, to Washington days before the
announcement seems likely to have been as accidental as the presence
in Mexico of Jesse Helms, head of the U.S. Foreign Affairs Committee,
during the Cuba vote crisis.

Taken together with the March 2002 U.S.-Mexico Border Partnership Plan, which shifted cross-border cooperation in the direction of
"smart borders," the security aftermath of 9-11 seemed set: More U.S.
pressures aimed at enlisting Mexico's security cooperation and more
Mexican—what? Historically, all the way to NAFTA, Mexico had always tried to bargain its cooperation with the U.S., but the fell swoop
of 9-11 took away its bargaining rights. What began as a give-take
strategy collapsed into unconditional concessions.

At that point, the other side of the Fox-Castañeda dilemma reared
itself in the shape of Mexican domestic politics. While U.S. foreign
policy went global after 9-11, for Mexico, the real story to the present
date is how foreign policy went domestic. It is hardly the stuff of myth,
yet full of lessons for a nonapocalyptic future. It is indeed, with its petty
chaining of would-be heroes and resolutely parochial determination
not to get caught up in foreign adventures, a story of the antiapocalyptic
spirit in action.

Castañeda was the first to burn his bridges with the Mexican public. It is hard to overestimate the reverberations within Mexico of his
dramatic decision to abandon a four-decade-long policy of friendly
communication with Cuba. Although rhetorically justified on the basis
of transition to democracy and Mexico's new "ethical" foreign policy,
the practical participation in the U.N. resolution condemning Cuba
had a clear U.S. imprint.[18] Equally startling, by any standards, was
Castañeda's gung-ho public response to 9-11, in which he claimed
that the U.S. had "every right and reason to seek revenge—we cannot
deny them support."[19] Only the crudeness of such an expression of
support is eloquent.

Behind such almost calculated, inept alignments to U.S. views and pressures, has been the deeper, but equally patent, failure of bilateralism to deliver more than unfulfilled promises and lingering frictions over undocumented migration, the participation of Mexican forces in international exercises, the government's quiescent reaction to the initiation of Northcom, and Cuba. The concomitant political tensions blew up in April 2002—again—when the PRI-dominated Senate denied President Fox permission to travel to the U.S. and Canada (a decision that Castañeda highlighted further by labeling it "anti-American"). Of more lasting significance, has been how mounting differences between the executive and the legislative branches over foreign policy matters have evolved to channel themselves into institutional expression. With regards to Cuba, the foreign minister's judgement was not only questioned in the press and the media, but also actively denounced by the opposition as a violation of the principle of nonintervention enshrined by article 89 of the Mexican Constitution. The initial petition by the Foreign Affairs Commission of both chambers, calling the executive to abstain in the vote against Cuba, turned into a polemic about the very constitutionality of Fox's foreign policy and the executive's prerogatives in the conduct of foreign policy itself.

This was also the case with Northcom. The defense commissions of both chambers have demanded that the government supply detailed information about the implications for Mexico of Northcom's creation. Members of the Senate have brought a constitutional challenge to the legality of potential foreign policy decisions, basing their case on Article 76 of the constitution, which requires the executive to obtain congressional approval to deploy troops beyond Mexico's frontiers.

The increasingly belligerent stance of opposition legislators, vis-à-vis the Fox administration's pursuit of a strongly pro-U.S. line, has taken the Mexican political debate all the way back to the founding constitutional principle of nonintervention and the prohibition of the threat or use of force in international relations—an unpromising principle for the prospects of security cooperation. The constitutional challenges already mounted suggest that Congress will play a more prominent part in forming future foreign policy. The range of actors who now have a claim to participate in foreign policymaking in Mexico has expanded in a kind of retribution for the administration's attempt to go it alone with the United States.

Seen from the outside, this may look bleak, not to say retrogressive. "Mexican backlash against democratic, pro-U.S. foreign policy" makes for an unkind headline north of the border. Is the opposition only a party political game? Some have argued that the constitution paper-waving has been mostly the result of self-promoting moves by the opposition intended for domestic political consumption. This line of reasoning maintains that such differences and tensions, particularly visible in the PRI-led Senate, are no more than the expression of democratization and the consequent politicization of Mexico's foreign policy.

However, it also could be maintained that these frictions point to a more fundamental disagreement over the wisdom of a policy of un-conditional concessions as the best course of action to deal with the northern neighbor. In this scenario, the deeper criticism of the Fox administration's handling of U.S. relations is that, in attempting to squash all alternative views (as Salinas did with NAFTA), it may have unnecessarily weakened Mexico's bargaining position. A concession made with much hand-wringing about the need to throw something to the almost insurmountable forces ranged against you is worth more than one made with no strings.

Fundamental disagreement about strategic relations with the U.S. may not ultimately involve a questioning of the need for those relations. But it can do serious damage to an administration that now stands accused of promising more than it can deliver, that is, overselling an upbeat assessment of Mexico's transition to democracy. Nowhere does this hit harder home in Mexico than in the area of jobs and migration. President Fox's promise to create one million jobs has not only not been fulfilled; during the past two years more than 500,000 jobs (mainly in border sweat shops and factories) also have been lost.[20] The need to secure a migratory agreement with the U.S.—one Mexican casualty of 9-11—has only intensified.

Here, the Fox administration finally seems to agree with its critics—and to be at loggerheads with the U.S. Mexico's position on the regular-ization of undocumented Mexicans has recently hardened, with a more vocal pursuit of the desecuritization of U.S. immigration policies. In a speech delivered at the League of United Latin American Citizens in Houston, the foreign minister denounced these policies as being par-tially responsible for the emergence of a significant "black and violent market" and for the levels of anarchy observed at the U.S.-Mexico border. As many had argued previously, Castañeda now insisted that order could only be recreated with a far-reaching agreeement aimed at regulating the interaction between "push and pull factors." This is not merely talk. Lack of progress in reaching such an agreement has not prevented the Mexican government from issuing consular identity cards to illegal migrants in the U.S., cards that more than sixty U.S. banks accept as guarantors for money transfers and remittances to Mexico.[21]

In a situation characterized by the inability of President Bush to make good on his expansive promises hinting at legalization, as well as by the open legitimation of undocumented labor exploitation embodied in the decision of the U.S. Supreme Court against José Castro, such moves become politically significant on a grand scale.[22] (The impasse here contrasts with the guest worker program implemented by Canada by which Mexican agricultural workers are paid Can. $7.10 an hour and have their labor rights protected.)[23] As Washington has tightened its immigration policy with a new law for border security, the path of cooperation now points to conflict.[24] When President Fox cancelled a trip to meet President Bush in Texas, in protest of the execution of Mexican Javier Suárez in August 2002, the bilateral relation appeared to be in trouble at the very highest levels. In newspaper declarations the same month, Fox was to be heard saying that, despite Mexico's unique trade relations with it, the U.S. does not appreciate Mexico as an equal partner.[25]

What is now coming from Mexico, in other words, is—after the backfire—the backlash. The Fox government may be only attempting to ride the tiger of popular opposition to its earlier strategies. Mexico, or more precisely, its foreign minister, may have been preparing for a backlash all along. Whatever the murky depths of the case, such moves as the abandonment of the Rio Treaty on September 6, 2002 are clearly designed to give the U.S. cause for concern. All the more symbolically so, since—besides its value to the U.S. as a means of guaranteeing hemisphereic security—the collective security provisions in the Rio Treaty were activated by Latin American states in the aftermath of 9-11. Nevertheless, the diplomatic words about cooperation from Mexico with new and old security risks will continue to flow toward the

United States. But beneath the words, it appears that Mexico is reaching a bottom line—one which might be expressed best numerically: In the last four years, more than 2,000 Mexicans and Central Americans who made it across the border have died in their impossible attempt to grasp the American Dream. With such a high price to pay for a security policy, this is a Mexican tragedy in the historical making.

Notes

1. Although security cooperation between Mexico and the U.S. remains understudied, the literature on the historical Mexican ambivalence toward the U.S. is extensive. Recent references, with a particular emphasis on the shift brought about by NAFTA and on the security dimension of the bilateral relation include Mónica Serrano, "Shifts in Mexican Foreign Policy" in Neil Harvey, (ed.), *Mexico: Dilemmas of Transition* (London: ILAS/British Academic Press, 1993); Mónica Serrano, "The Armed Branch of the State: Civil-Military Relations in Mexico," *Journal of Latin American Studies* 27, no. 2; Manau Raul Benítez, "Sovereignty, Foreign Policy, and National Security in Mexico 1821–1989" in H. P. Klepak (ed.), *Natural Allies? Canadian and Mexican Perspectives on International Security* (Ottawa: Carleton University, 1996); Guadalupe González and Stephan Haggard, "The United States and Mexico: A Pluralistic Security Community?" in E. Adler and M. Barnett (eds.), *Security Communities* (Cambridge, U.K.: Cambridge University, 1998); Francisco Valdés-Ugalde, "Janus and the Northern Colossus: Perceptions of the United States in the Building of the Mexican Nation," *The Journal of America History* 86, no. 2 (September 1999): 568–600; Susana Chacón, "La negociación del acuerdo militar entre México y los Estados Unidos, 1940–1942," *Foro Internacional* 40, no. 2 (April–June 2000): 307–344; Jorge Domínguez Jorge and Rafael Fernández de Castro, *The United States and Mexico* (New York: Routledge, 2001).
2. In a press conference published on November 4, 2001, President Fox called for the three countries to work together toward a "North American Security Policy" aimed at coordinating border policies and to increased sharing of immigration and customs information. "From 'Open Borders' to 'Code Red'," *PSI Global Affairs Report*, no. 4 (November 2001).
3. The reorganization of the national defense system, with the integration of the navy, and new procurements, was also the result of these bilateral security efforts. Notwithstanding this, the extent of actual cooperation was limited. Only 165 members of the armed forces received special training in U.S. military academies, while the Joint Defense Commission met formally only a couple of times in 1942. Chacón, "La negociación," 340–342.
4. Clark, W. Reynolds and S. Wager, "Integración económica de México y Estados Unidos. Implicaciones para la seguridad de ambos países," in Sergio Aguayo and Bruce M. Bagley (eds.), *En Busca de la Seguridad*

Perdida (México City: Siglo XXI, 1990); Chacón, La "negociación," 311–337.

5. For a more detailed analysis of U.S.-Mexico cooperation on nuclear nonproliferation, see Mónica Serrano, *Common Security in Latin America: The 1967 Treaty of Tlatelolco* (London: Institute of Latin American Studies, 1992).

6. Between 1990 and 1999, exports among these three countries increased at an average rate of around 10.9 percent, from U.S. $229.9 billion to a total of U.S. $585.51 billion. During these years, Mexico and Canada also emerged as each other's third largest trading partner. In terms of job creation, the number of jobs lost due to the NAFTA effect pale in comparison with the more than 20 million jobs created in the U.S. between 1993 and 1999. Similarly, the flows of Foreign Direct Investment running through these economies have revealed an impressively dynamic trend. See Robert Pastor, *Toward a North American Community: Lessons from the Old World to the New* (Washington D.C.: Institute for International Economics, 2001): 66–73.

7. Stephen D. Morris, "Reforming the Nation: Mexican Nationalism in Context," *Journal of Latin American Studies* 31, no. 2 (May 1999). According to Morris, it was the favorable public perception of closer economic integration that ultimately prompted the ruling elite to modify its traditional discourse toward the U.S.

8. See Kate Doyle, "The militarization of the drug-war in Mexico," *Current History* 92 (1993): 571; Timothy J. Dunn, *The Militarization of the U.S.-México Border, 1978–1992* (Austin: University of Texas Press); Peter Andreas, "Free-Market Reform and Drug-Market Prohibition: U.S. Policies at Cross Purposes in Latin America," *Third World Quarterly* 16, no. 1 (1995).

9. Dunn, *Militarization*; Martha L. Cottam and Otwin Marenin, "International Cooperation in the War on Drugs: Mexico and the United States," *Policing and Society* 9 (1999): 209–240.

10. For this and the following, see Mónica Serrano and Maria Celia Toro, "From Drug-Trafficking to Transnational Organised Crime in Latin America" in Mats Berdal and Mónica Serrano (eds.), *Transnational Organised Crime and International Security: Business as Usual?* (Boulder, Colo. and London: Lynne Rienner, 2002); Robert J. MacCoun and Peter Reuter, *Drug War Heresies: Learning from Other Vices, Times and Places* (Cambridge, U.K.: Cambridge University Press, 2001).

11. For this and the following, see José Z. García, "Security Regimes on the U.S.-Mexico Border" in John Bailey and Jorge Chabat (eds.), *Transnational Crime and Public Security: Challenges to Mexico and the United States* (La Jolla, Cal.: Center for U.S.-Mexican Studies, University of California, San Diego, 2002); William F. McDonald, "Mexico, the U.S. and the Migration-Crime Nexus" in ibid; see also "Reportan aumento de muertes en Arizona," *Reforma*, June 29, 2002.

12. Doris Meissner, "Two Jobs for One INS," *The Washington Post*, March 28, 2002; Demetrois G. Papademetriou, "An Immigration and National Security Grand Bargain with Mexico," paper prepared for the

international seminar on "National Security, Border Security, Migration, and Human Rights," Sin Fronteras, El Colegio de la Frontera Norte and El Colegio de México, Mexico City, April 7–9, 2002.

13. For an analysis of the Grupo Beta, see García, "Security Regimes"; and McDonald, "Mexico, the U.S."

14. See, for example, the views expressed by environmentalist Ben Zuckerman for the American perception of the Mexican border as a place of pollution and overpopulation, reported in Bata Sergio Muñoz, "Prometen legalizar a indocumentados," *Reforma*, August 1, 2002.

15. See "Reconoce Castañeda la fuerza hegemónica de E.U. Plantea SRE conciliar principios e intereses," *Reforma*, June 28, 2002.

16. See "Bush dice que la relación con México es lo más importante para E.U.," *El País*, September 6, 2001.

17. Rafael de Castro Fernández, "Seguridad y fronteras en América del Norte," *Reforma*, June 10, 2002.

18. See Raymundo Rivapalacio, "Más allá del voto cubano," *Milenio Diario*, April 16, 2001; "Reconoce México violaciones en Cuba," *Reforma*, April 18, 2001; "Rechaza el Senado respaldar la postura," *Reforma*, April 19, 2001; "Ataca Cuba a Castañeda," *Reforma*, April 21, 2001; "Señala Cuba a Castañeda como promotor de censura," *Uno Más Uno*, April 21, 2001.

19. See "Fair-weather friends?" *The Economist* 360, no. 8240, September 22, 2001.

20. See *Reforma*, September 1, 2002.

21. See *Uno Más Uno*, August 30, 2002.

22. Reviewing the dispute between a Mexican undocumented employee and the Hoffman Plastic Compounds, the U.S. Supreme Court resolved on March 27, 2002, that undocumented workers in the U.S. have no labor rights. The implications of such a decision become clear if we take into account that at least 60 percent of the labor force in California's labor intensive agriculture (or 30 percent of U.S. agricultural production) relies on undocumented Mexican workers. This is a reality that has been openly acknowledged by the U.S. Department of Labor, and indeed by the calls by some governors of U.S. Southern border states, including Jane Hull of Arizona, for a return to a temporary guest workers program to permit agricultural workers entry visas to the U.S. See Bustamante, 2001 and 2002; see also García, "Security Regimes," 329.

23. Interviews with farm workers reported in the press confirm a positive view held both by the Canadian and Mexican governments. See "Da acuerdo con Canada seguridad a jornaleros," *Reforma*, June 29, 2002.

24. See Jorge A. Bustamante, "Cuestión de dignidad nacional," *Milenio Diario*, April 1, 2002; and "Endurece Bush control migratorio," *Reforma*, May 15, 2002.

25. *Uno Más Uno*, August 30, 2002; *El País*, August 29, 2002.

4

THE VIEW FROM THE ATTIC

Toward a Gated Continental Community?[1]

STEPHEN CLARKSON

The catastrophe suffered by Americans on September 11, 2001 resonated around the world, raising questions about both the security and economic consequences for every country's relationship with the global hegemon. These issues had their most powerful impact on the United States' two neighbors, causing each country to revert to earlier patterns of behavior. To the south, Mexico reaffirmed its aversion to American military might and lost the intimate access in the Washington hierarchy that its new president seemed on the point of securing. To the north, a long history of deep military and economic integration between Canada and the United States evoked reflexes of close cooperation.

From the point of view of the United States's largest trading partner, its most dependent military-strategic partner, and its only contiguous neighbor along its northern borders, this chapter looks at three issues: the *military* response to the attacks, the *societal* dimension of the ensuing counterterrorism effort, and the *economic* implications of both types of reaction.

What differentiated Canada's response—whether the debate in the public domain or the actual policy moves made by the federal government—from other countries' reactions was the set of special problems generated by sharing a common border with the U.S. and a longstanding military partnership. Canada presents a special internal security concern to Washington because its 5,525–mile border constitutes the United States's longest with another state and more than 500,000 people cross the Canada-U.S. border's 425 crossing points each day.[2] But with $1.9 billion worth of daily trade—that is, 82 percent of Canada's exports and 71 percent of its imports—crossing the boundary largely by truck, the same border causes Canada an acute concern about its economic security.[3] Any measure that slows trade in the interests of security simultaneously confronts the increasingly integrated Canadian-American economic system with a serious liability.

Initial policy responses in Ottawa to this double problematic veered from one extreme to another. More complacent Canadian observers held that nothing had changed on September 11, except that the human calamity suffered by workers in the twin towers and the Pentagon, as well as by the passengers on United Airlines Flight 93, had brought Americans into the club of the vulnerable to which the rest of the world already belonged. Those suicide missions were only spectacular dramatizations of globalization's dark side. Relentless bombings in Northern Ireland through the 1990s, the indiscriminate violence of the Red Brigades in Italy in the 1980s, and even the occasional killings effected by the Front de Libération du Québec in Montreal up to 1970 reminded the public that terrorism has been a scourge ravaging various societies at different moments. As for the anti-American rage seething throughout the Arab world, "jihad" already had entered everyday vocabulary, signifying a martyr-led holy war that Muslims might wage against the imperialist infidel.

In this non-alarmist optic, the Americans now had experienced for themselves the destructive power of a small group whose technical sophistication and discreet fanaticism can elude detection even by technologically superior intelligence agencies. Al Qaeda's coup certainly showed that security measures and intelligence capabilities would need to be improved in Canada, in close conjunction with every other state, but it was the United States, whose immigration and intelligence failures had been demonstrated by the terrorists' freedom of movement on American soil, that needed to make the greatest changes.

Such northern smugness was dismissed by the more paranoid in Canada when Washington, in its alarm, caused traffic gridlock at customs posts and panic in boardrooms by temporarily closing down its northern border. According to this view, if Canada were ever to regain an open economic border with the U.S., it would have to pursue a degree of military integration with the United States that was even greater than what it had known during the hand-in-glove decades of the Cold War's anti-Soviet aerospace defense. One way or another, Canada would now also need to integrate its land and sea forces within the Americans' command structure.

The Military: Armed Reaction to Sabotage

This acceptance of full support for the American response to Islamic terrorism came naturally to the Canadian military, because it was simply a restatement of the long-established North American defense relationship. Back in the late 1930s, when the hitherto unthinkable threats to North America from Nazi Germany and Imperial Japan were actually becoming thinkable, the president of the United States and the prime minister of Canada formulated the principles that defined how they would cope with common security threats. In a speech in Kingston, Ontario, on August 18, 1938, Franklin Delano Roosevelt declared that even the neutral American people "would not stand idly by" if Canada was attacked. William Lyon Mackenzie King responded with his own declaration two days later in the sleepy town of Woodbridge outside Toronto to the effect that "enemy forces should not be able to pursue their way either by land, sea or air to the United States across Canadian territory."

The North American military integration initiated during World War II after these declarations of mutual responsibility continued to develop during the Cold War. Canada chose to be a target for Soviet nuclear bombs or missiles because it had taken the lead in creating the North Atlantic Treaty Organization (NATO), a multilateral peacetime security organization under Washington's leadership dedicated to containing the communist threat. For the next four decades, Canadian leaders endorsed whatever strategic doctrine on nuclear retaliation the Pentagon might issue as it responded to new circumstances and incorporated its military-industrial complex's latest technologies.

Blending Canada into a single system was effected militarily by the North American Air (now Aerospace) Defense Command (NORAD), which was set up in 1958 to counter the Soviet bomber and missile threat by integrating under the U.S. Air Force's Strategic Air Command the Royal Canadian Air Force's interceptors, its nuclear-tipped Bomarc missiles, and the U.S.-built and operated Distant Early Warning radar system located in the Canadian arctic.

The Defense Production Sharing Agreements (DPSA) of 1957 institutionalized the economic counterpart of Canada's strategic integration for the Cold War at the same time. Through DPSA, the Canadian defense industry, which was largely comprised of American branch plants, gained privileged access to Pentagon contracts to produce the requisite weaponry using leading-edge technology. From Washington's point of view, the decentralization of some defense production to Canada made the American military production system less vulnerable to Soviet attack.

There were several corollaries to this picture of happy continental cooperation. If Canadians did not want the U.S. taking over their airspace, they had to invest enough resources to do the job to the Pentagon's satisfaction, a stance known to military analysts as "Defense against Help." Eager to oblige, the Canadian armed forces lobbied for the armaments necessary for them to participate actively within the U.S.-defined parameters. For its part, the cost-conscious government of Canada quietly resisted continual pressure from the Pentagon to spend more on its military.

Immediate, post-catastrophe behavior on both sides of the 49th parallel in the autumn of 2001 seemed to confirm that the Cold War still provided the template for the Canadian-American security relationship. In the event, it turned out to fit operations abroad rather than continental defense. George W. Bush's declaration of war against terrorism connected Canada to the state of global affairs that had existed before the Berlin Wall came down in 1989, namely a war that rallied the forces of light against an evil, if invisible, empire. In this apocalyptic spirit, Prime Minister Jean Chrétien immediately endorsed the Bush Doctrine and offered his armed forces for the execution of the United States's military attack against the Taliban government of Afghanistan and its associated terrorist organization, Al Qaeda, assumed to have planned the September 11 attack.

Least controversial was the Canadian government's sending a Canadian Navy task group of two frigates, a destroyer, and a supply ship to work in conjunction with the allied fleet in the Arabian Sea.[4] Canadian warships had experience in operating under American command since their coordination in antisubmarine patrols during World War II. Prime Minister Brian Mulroney had sent frigates to support the American fleet in the Gulf War with no adverse results.[5]

Ottawa's decision in early 2002 to send 750 Canadian soldiers from the Princess Patricia's Light Infantry Regiment to be deployed in the Kandahar area as part of a U.S. Army task force raised more difficult questions. Why, for instance, if Canada was so eager to participate in the military action in Afghanistan, had it not joined the multinational security force that had been organized by the British? The answer appeared to be that the Canadian military had been rebuffed by Europe, which asked them to provide a field laundry unit and then engineers. Stung by this European slight, the Chrétien government felt valued by the Americans who, with only Humvees on the ground in Afghanistan, said they would welcome its forces' more formidable Coyotes, armored vehicles designed and manufactured by General Motors in Ontario.[6]

Canadian troops fighting with the U.S. military had a history. In Bosnia and Kosovo, they were part of multilateral forces under United Nations or NATO mandates.[7] In Afghanistan, however, they were to be fully integrated under U.S. command, a situation that delighted some. Art Eggleton, the Canadian minister of defense, was visibly—some felt embarrassingly—excited to be included in a U.S. mission, as if the boys had been invited to join the men. "This is the first time," he said, "that the Americans have asked a coalition ally to join them on the ground with their operations in Afghanistan . . . This is the first time they have done that for any country, and they asked Canada first."[8]

Others in Canada were appalled at the implications for Canadian treaty obligations of fighting *for* rather than just *with* the Americans who had already decided not to abide by the Geneva Convention on the treatment of prisoners of war. Claiming that the Taliban or Al Qaeda fighters they captured were not legitimate soldiers, the Pentagon whisked their "detainees" off for interrogation to concentration camps in Guantanamo Bay, Cuba. A furor broke out in Parliament when it was revealed that the Canadian contingent was indeed handing over its prisoners to the American military, since it would be impossible to guarantee they would be treated according to international law.

Consternation spilled out from the House of Commons into the whole of the country on the night of April 18, when an American pilot, guided by his high-tech monitoring system on a nighttime patrol, managed to mistake the Canadian platoon for the enemy and dropped a bomb that killed four Canadian soldiers. To this appalling injury, the U.S. president added gratuitous insult. Despite five public appearances the next day, George W. Bush failed to offer condolences to the people of Canada or to the families of the bereaved—in marked contrast to his effusions when three U.S. soldiers were killed by similar "friendly fire" four months before. Following a statement of dismay from Deputy Prime Minister John Manley, Bush offered an apology the next day, leaving Canadians feeling irrelevant and snubbed.[9]

Although Afghanistan's social infrastructure was in ruins, the government of Canada chose not to exploit its strength in peace-building that focuses on reconstructing a civil society from the devastation of war. Because sending soldiers to fight under another belligerent's flag ran counter to major traditions in Canadian foreign policy, we may infer that concern for Afghanistan was not the main story. Had the Chrétien government held this far-off land's welfare to its heart rather than calculating its own interests, it would not have sent troops. In offering to do America's dirty—and, as it turned out, deadly—work in the mopping-up phase of its high-tech bombing war, the Chrétien government was sending an obvious signal to Washington. Integrating its forces in the U.S. military machine sent the message to the White House that Canada was fully on board. Ottawa's main priority was not peace in Afghanistan. It was pleasing, calming, and influencing Uncle Sam in a situation starkly different from and, politically speaking, far more threatening than the Cold War.

The Societal: Countering a Transsocietal Problem

In the nuclear standoff with the USSR, the United States's continental defense perimeter extended to its Canadian protectorate's Arctic frontier, where it installed radar stations to detect possible Soviet attacks. The threat was military, distant, and external to both the hegemon and its northern neighbor. This left the common Canada-U.S. border as a traditional interstate barrier whose economic height was determined by relatively low tariffs and whose human height was set by comparatively permissive immigration and tourist regulations.

In this new war, the largest change in the nature of the threat was in the anthropology of the enemy. Like any leading state, the U.S. always had concerns about spies from the other side seeking secret information or carrying out sabotage during wartime, whether hot or cold. Now the threat was less from visible states than from nonstate actors with their networks of destructive capacity cunningly embedded throughout the industrialized world's multicultural mosaic. From what was known about Al Qaeda's training camps and the machinations that culminated on September 11, Americans had to assume that "sleepers" continued to go about their otherwise normal daily routines in all countries. Some could be illegal immigrants, but others would have their papers in order, holding down steady jobs, dating white women or men, and fathering—or perhaps mothering—in interracial households. They could even be full-fledged citizens professing they loved America as much as Allah. So the United States' most dangerous enemies were not necessarily lurking in a Himalayan redoubt, but going about their business unrecognizable within their multiracial communities in Florida or in France.

In this novel context, it was not clear against what threat to the United States Canada was now supposed to assure the defense of its territory. Once it was bombed out of Afghanistan, Al Qaeda presented no military danger to the U.S. heartland. Nor was any rogue, axis-of-evil state's army, navy, or air force credibly able to threaten North America. This absence of a traditional defense problem did not prevent some Canadians, including leading figures in the armed forces, from arguing that the new realities revealed on September 11 required not just the extension of NORAD to include control of the eventual National Missile Defense System, but also the complete integration of Canada's naval and army services within their American counterparts.[10]

This was a Canadian solution in search of a not-yet-existent American need. Evidence that the White House was not exercised about its Canadian connections could be seen in the proposed Office of Homeland Security, whose mandate was to reorganize domestic institutions, not coordinate with those of its NAFTA partners. The proof that the

Pentagon was not particularly concerned with a military threat coming through Canada was apparent in its proposed structure for "homeland" defense. True, Northern Command, which was to integrate the U.S. military's four famously autonomous services under one headquarters, would be responsible within the Pentagon for North American defense, a region that included Mexico and Canada.

Since the new command was expected to be joined with NORAD's, Canada's junior partnership in the latter could draw it partially into the former.[11] If the Canadian government had been under pressure to extend continental military cooperation from aerospace to integrated land and sea command structures, it probably would have required a commitment of resources at a certain level of readiness.[12] Worse, in the speculation of analyst Michael Byers, U.S. generals might be tempted to keep their own troops out of harm's way, preferring to use Canadians for the more dangerous missions.[13] But Northcom's formal mandate was only to "cooperate" with its neighbors' armed forces. Taken at its face value, this would mean that the reorganized American military's domestic mission was not to integrate with, let alone displace, the Canadian military.

In the new logic of Islamic terrorism, Canada found itself a target for two reasons. It was directly vulnerable to Al Qaeda's retribution because Ottawa's policies to the Middle East leaned distinctly in Israel's favor. Once it rallied to support Washington's military campaign against Afghanistan as the haven for bin Laden, it had to consider itself a hated crusader by association. As a primary target in its own right, Canada had to look to its own defenses against terrorism. As a potential staging area for insinuating operatives into the United States, Canada played a secondary role in American counterterrorism. Consequently, Ottawa's nonmilitary policy response to September 11 was driven both by domestic and by American demands for security against terror. Between these two pressures on Canadian policy there was some common ground and some divergence.

The domestic demands involving Canadian security were not substantially different from those that governments overseas faced in dealing with increased threat levels from terrorism. With the globalization of interdependence, domestic security had become transnationalized. As was the case with other states, Canada's own security perimeter now extended to every visa office, seaport, and international airport—whether Heathrow, Charles de Gaulle, Frankfurt, or Tokyo—from which dangerous weapons could be shipped or potential terrorists could arrive, presenting themselves as immigrants, refugees who had lost or destroyed their documents, or innocent-looking tourists with dollars to spend on sightseeing in the Rockies. Defense against terrorism therefore required a generalized sharing of data among intelligence services using the latest technologies for trying to ferret out the dangerous and then tracking their movements. The role of the military was secondary in this effort of transsocietal sleuthing. Primary was the work of immigration, customs, intelligence, and police forces cooperating globally to detect the planning and then prevent the execution of horrific sabotage.

The United States signaled very mixed demands on its protectorate for counterterrorist security. Wildly inaccurate statements by politicians, public figures, and media pundits gave some observers the impression that Washington would force Ottawa to harmonize its relevant policies to U.S. standards or face the consequence of a barricaded border. A congenitally misinformed Congress alarmed by panicky media—which were fed by too-smart-by-half pundits, themselves chronically ignorant about Canada—generated continual political turbulence about the security of the United States's northern border. Former Clinton ambassador to the United Nations, Richard Holbrooke's earlier remark that Canada was "a Club Med for terrorists" was recycled. One TV program, "America's Most Wanted," defied both the evidence and the Canadian embassy's frantic denials to claim that all nineteen highjackers had entered the United States through Canada. Even freshman Senator Hillary Clinton, who should have known better, stated that the terrorists came to the U.S. through Canada. Confirming the U.S. media's general ignorance and contributing to the public's misinformation about the territory to their north, the popular TV series "The West Wing" even referred in one episode to terrorists crossing the (nonexistent) Ontario-Vermont border.

Confounding this image of mortal threat from the north was the spontaneous response of real Canadians, whether in their homes or in their professional capacities. Immediate was the welcome extended by Canadian communities to passengers who were stranded for days until they could resume or retrace their journeys. On September 11, when

Washington shut down American air space, 224 airliners carrying 33,000 passengers were diverted to Canadian airports. Halifax received 40 diverted planes with 8,000 passengers, St. John's, Newfoundland 27 flights and 4,400 passengers. Gander, a Newfoundland town of some ten thousand souls, took in 6,595 passengers from 38 aircraft and converted schools, meeting halls, and other gathering places into mass lodging areas with cots and sleeping bags. Seventy-seven members of the Canadian Red Cross's disaster response team left their regular jobs in nursing, firefighting, or counseling to work three-week shifts in the ruins of Ground Zero. High-rigging Mohawks from the Aboriginal Oka reserve in Quebec joined with some 200 other Canadian ironworkers to help dismantle the World Trade Center's structure.[14]

The Canadian government's signals were more mixed. Despite Chrétien's instantly offered expressions of sympathy and the government's quickly organized mass demonstration on Parliament Hill to express public solidarity with the victims, the prime minister was outshone by his British counterpart. In setting the standard for unreserved, even embarrassing cheerleading for President Bush, Prime Minister Tony Blair (who brilliantly outflanked the opposition Tories on his American front so that, presumably, he could take Britain into Euroland) made the Canadian prime minister's support appear reluctant. When President Bush failed to mention Canada in the thanks he expressed to American allies in his speech before Congress, the hypersensitive media in Canada instantly concluded that he had snubbed Chrétien for foot dragging.

Such appearances were deceptive. Chrétien's public reserve was consistent with his reluctance to be perceived—as had his predecessor, the Conservative Brian Mulroney—as an American lapdog. In suggesting that September 11 had not radically changed the parameters of the military danger or the subversive threat posed by terrorism, he appeared to endorse positions expressed by the complacent. However, in acting backstage with energetic resolve to transform Canada's security stance, his government showed it was closer to the views of the alarmist who insisted that the acid test for Canada would be Washington's satisfaction that Ottawa and the provinces were doing what it defined as necessary. This was the "Defense against Help" doctrine in antiterrorist dress.

At the logical limit, the U.S. government's confidence in Canadian reliability would only be achieved by the complete harmonization of the two countries' practices and the full integration of their personnel and data gathering. Under this model, the question about which country's norms would determine the common standard seemed to have an obvious answer. But it took only a moment's reflection to reject the apparently obvious. Canadians would surely not agree to lower their gun control standards to the U.S. level since this would increase, not decrease, their domestic insecurity.

Full policy harmonization would also weaken Canadian refugee and immigration procedures that had proved more effective at monitoring terrorists than had those of their American counterparts.[15] In 1996, Canada had pioneered an immigration control system, which put officers in airports abroad where they had stopped more than 33,000 people with false documents before they boarded planes bound for North America.[16] As a result, immigration security in Canada was considered tougher than in the U.S. According to Janet Dench, executive director of the Canadian Council for Refugees, "about half of refugee claimants come through the U.S. because they know it's easier to get into."[17] Exporting U.S. practices and North-Americanizing the insecurity that characterized American society—including the ease with which Al Qaeda's plotters could train at flight schools—would clearly be retrograde. After all, it was not the Canadian Security and Intelligence Service, but the FBI and CIA, which were responsible for the evident collapse of American security and intelligence that admitted the September 11 terrorists and failed to prevent them from highjacking four airliners on the fateful morning.[18]

Within the understandably heated debates around these issues, the American ambassador to Canada was an important voice of reasoned calm. As articulated by Paul Cellucci, the issue was how to achieve mutual confidence. When translated from diplomatese, this meant the issue was gaining informed American confidence in Canadian procedures. Standards for accepting desirable immigrants and procedures for dispatching dangerous applicants could be the same or different as long as they were effective. A process of intense, often tense, bilateral discussions among officials took place through the autumn, with Canadian officials explaining their practices to their predictably overbearing but frequently less expert U.S. colleagues.

The known implantation in all liberal capitalist societies of networked terrorist cells in a formal state of jihad did not require new policies as much as strengthening existing laws and putting more state resources behind their implementation. Draft legislation or amendments that discriminated more sharply between the desirable and the dangerous and that ensured rejected applicants would be expelled from the country had been in the parliamentary pipeline well before September. The federal government accordingly proceeded to strengthen Canada's internal counterterrorism capacity on various fronts, many of which implemented the country's international obligations detailed in treaties that Ottawa had helped negotiate:

- It reinforced the security around potential targets for economic sabotage and social disruption.
- It amended the Immigration Act to allow the suspension or termination of refugee determination proceedings if there were reasonable grounds to believe a claimant was a terrorist, a war criminal, or a senior official of a government engaged in terrorist activities.[19]
- It addressed the security of Canadian skies by amendments to the Aeronautics Act that strengthened security requirements for the design or construction of aircraft, airports, and facilities; tightened screening of people and goods entering restricted areas; made it an offense to engage in any behavior endangering the safety or security of a flight or persons on board; and required air carriers or those operating aviation reservation systems to provide basic information on specific passengers or flights when requested for security purposes.
- It made improvements to checking the background on immigration applicants made by the visa office in Canadian embassies.
- It tightened controls on funds flowing through legitimate financial institutions to suspect networks. By mid-December, Canadian financial institutions had frozen $344,000 associated with twenty-two accounts designated under the U.N. Suppression of Terrorism Regulations. The government of Canada invested $63 million in a Financial Transaction Reports Analysis Centre to interdict funds flowing to terrorists.[20]

Some new legislation was also introduced. Bill C-36, the Anti-Terrorism Act, which became law on December 18, 2001, defined terrorist activity so broadly that civil liberties and ethnic groups protested it could be used to suppress legitimate political dissent: "any action, taken to achieve a political or religious purpose, that harms people, endangers life, health or safety, disrupts essential services or damages property in a manner that causes bodily harm or threats to life, health or safety." It decreed tougher sentences for terrorism offenses; made it a crime knowingly to participate in, facilitate, fund, or contribute to a terrorist group; eased the use of electronic surveillance against terrorist groups; and within carefully defined limits, allowed the preventive arrest and detention of suspected terrorists and the compulsion of information from people with information about terrorists.[21] A new Immigration and Refugee Protection Act became law on June 28, 2002, to introduce higher penalties for immigration offenses and declare violators of international human rights, members of organized crime syndicates, and other security threats ineligible for refugee status.[22]

A year later, it seems apparent that the measures taken by the Canadian government to beef up security were used primarily to reassure the U.S. government that Canada was not in fact a terrorist mecca, and to send the message, through the new Immigration and Refugee Protection Act, that Canada was no longer a "soft-touch" for prospective immigrants.[23] Indeed, the most severe provisions of this new legislation, such as detaining suspects without charges, had not been used by September 11, 2002.

While it might have been expected that Ottawa would resist committing as much as the U.S. government wanted it to spend on counterterrorism and border security, Finance Minister Paul Martin's fall budget allocated Can. $7.7 billion for five years to the various terrorist control and border maintenance programs, a sum proportionately larger than the U.S. allocation to the same objectives:

- $1.6 billion for intelligence and policing;
- $1 billion to improve screening of visitors, immigrants, and refugee claimants;
- $1.6 billion to double the capacity of Joint Task Force Two, which supported Canada's military participation in the war on

terrorism and its ability to respond to chemical, biological, and nuclear threats;

- $2.2 billion to make air travel more secure by arming air marshals, training guards who screen passengers and baggage, introducing explosive detection systems at airports, and enhancing security at airports; and
- $1.2 billion for border related measures, including $646 million for enhancing boundary security with new information-sharing technology that screens goods and travelers while facilitating traffic flows between Canada and the United States.[24]

As Ottawa saw it, the government of Canada actually set the bilateral agenda on these border issues because it had done its homework long before September 11 and because it was institutionally more nimble than the U.S. government. For years it had been urging Washington to undertake joint measures that would improve border security (detecting dangerous immigrants) and increase border efficiency (speeding the passage of reliable cargoes while directing border personnel to concentrate on higher risk shipments). Canada-U.S. border partnership talks had been initiated with the Clinton administration, but had made little progress. When September 11 finally caused the U.S. government to take the issue seriously, Ottawa had coherent plans ready to propose, for example, Integrated Border Enforcement Teams and fraud-resistant permanent identity cards for new immigrants.

The Canadian counterpart to former Pennsylvania governor Tom Ridge, whom Bush appointed to coordinate his administration's action on homeland security, was Foreign Minister John Manley, whom the prime minister assigned as point man on Canada-U.S. security relations after September 11. Whereas Ridge took months to get his act together, the centralization inherent in parliamentary government gave Manley immediate command over all the federal government's relevant programs and officials.

As a result, the Canadian embassy in Washington could claim that the bulk of the 30-Point Smart Border Action Plan signed by Ridge and Manley in December was Canadian, although the stationing of U.S. customs inspectors in major Canadian seaports, which act as transshipment depots for cargoes heading for the United States, was clearly a Washington demand. Vital points of the Smart Border Initiative included developing secure preclearance procedures for both commercial transactions and regular cross-border commuters to speed border traffic, visa policy coordination, compatible immigration databases to operate in real time, and many infrastructure improvements.[25]

On September 9, 2002, Jean Chrétien and George W. Bush held a summit at the Ambassador Bridge on the Detroit-Windsor, Ontario border, the busiest crossing on the continent, to discuss the progress made so far. Both leaders endorsed improving infrastructure to speed cross-border traffic. They witnessed demonstrations of FAST, a preclearance system for frequent commercial traffic such as auto parts shipments and of NEXUS, a revived program for preclearing frequent cross-border commuters.[26]

Measures announced to satisfy the government's two publics— its electorate at home and the hegemon in Washington—raised the perennial question of Canadian sovereignty. Clearly, what Uncle Sam wanted, Uncle Sam got. But if the Canadian public agreed with its government in wanting the same heightened levels of security, little autonomy had actually been sacrificed.

The Supreme Court's unanimous ruling in January 2002 to allow the deportation of an Iranian assassin on the grounds of national security strengthened the government's case in Washington that Canada was not a safe haven for terrorists. When Prime Minister Chrétien separated the security functions from the Department of Foreign Affairs and International Trade and left them in the hands of John Manley, he reinforced this message. By promoting Manley to be deputy prime minister, Chrétien gave maximum governmental authority to the man in his cabinet for whom the Bush administration had the greatest trust. He also signaled not only how completely Canada had moved into an intimate partnership with Washington, but also that the process of responding to American demands for the integration of selected policy fronts would continue quietly on a piecemeal basis, one low-profile issue at a time.

In this delicate situation, the president was less of an asset to Ottawa than was his political team. The advantage for Canada of "Dubya" surrounding himself with older, but experienced Republican alumni was the familiarity of Donald Rumsfeld and Dick Cheney with Canada from Cold War days. With those connections to NATO and NORAD and with Secretary of State Colin Powell's greater proclivity for moderation, apocalyptic scenarios in which Canada had to sacrifice its sovereignty to gain admission to Fortress Bush seemed far-fetched. Nevertheless, the nature of a post-catastrophe North American economy remained to be redefined.

The Economic: NAFTA Plus or NAFTA Minus?

The post-September 11 future of the continental economy that had been institutionalized in 1994 by the North American Free Trade Agreement (NAFTA) appeared to depend on how the U.S. government approached its security imperative along its territorial borders. Under NAFTA, the already advanced level of integration between the United States and its two peripheral economies had been proceeding under conditions of political separation, without institutions for collective governance. The corporate management paradigm on which the single North American market was premised, such as just-in-time production, was in jeopardy once Washington's national vision switched from an expansive growth strategy to a defensive security stance.

From Canada's point of view, two-way trade had doubled since the original bilateral free trade agreement had been signed on January 1, 1989, supporting millions of jobs in each country but increasing the economy's vulnerability to border blockages. The day after Washington virtually closed down the Canadian border, trucks were backed up more than 15 miles from the U.S. border in Ontario.[27]

If a new Fortress America were to be constructed from the ashes of Ground Zero, the issue for both Canada and Mexico would be the location of the ramparts. If these customs and immigration fortifications were to be a new Hadrian's Wall along the United States's territorial boundaries, then the St. Lawrence River, the Great Lakes, and the Rio Grande would become the moats across which the two peripheral states looked in tortured frustration at their once-promised market.

In this gated-nation scenario, September 11 sidelined President Vicente Fox's agenda for legalizing the status of all Mexican migrants in the U.S.—shortly after he seemed to have gained general support in Bush's Washington. Mexicans' historically determined reluctance to endorse a U.S. military campaign against a Third-World country pushed Mexico City off the administration's policy horizon for the ensuing year.[28]

If stiffened border control measures significantly slowed the flow of Canadian exports, the painful restructuring provoked by trade and investment liberalization would not only have been suffered in vain, but also would have turned into a monumental disaster with an impact north of the border no less calamitous than the destruction of New York's twin trade towers. Plants, whose production could be used only when integrated with operations in the U.S. or Mexico, would close. Canadians would learn once more the lesson that Richard Nixon tried to teach them in 1971: There are high risks to any economy built on the principle of continental economic integration, which does not have parallel political institutions that allow it to participate in formulating the hegemon's policies.

The prospect of the U.S. border staffed by legions of National Guard, customs, and immigration officials suggested a reprise of the isolation-ism instituted in 1930 by the huge tariffs of the Smoot-Hawley Act. An elementary realism called on Canadians to take such a retroscenario se-riously. The historical default position for Canadian governments had been to maximize continental integration in the belief that prosperity would be enhanced by participation in the larger American market. The Dominion of Canada's first and greatest prime minister, John A. Macdonald, only introduced his National Policy in 1879—to promote a more autonomous Canadian economy that would develop on an east-west basis—when he had failed to persuade post-bellum Washington to reinstitute the reciprocity agreement it had abrogated during the Civil War. Pierre Trudeau only sanctioned the "Third Option" strat-egy to reduce Canadian vulnerability to the vagaries of American policy when Nixon jacked up economic barriers in 1971. In short, Canadians have traditionally wanted in, with Washington deciding whether to open or close the door to them.

If history suggested that Canada's economic fate was in the hands of the United States, was it not for the post-catastrophe hyperpower to decide whether Canada was to be defined inside or outside its de-fense perimeter? Yes and No. "Washington" was not a unitary actor free to do whatever it liked. The NAFTA-bred situation of increased economic interdependence generated material interests on the part of American firms who relied on open borders. These corporations wielded significant political and economic power, thereby constraining Washington's options. Cold War continental decentralization of strategic industries had spawned American companies that obligingly developed substantial branch operations in Canada, and therefore had an interest in not losing their investments to the excessive zeal of the border police. Under free trade, many U.S. transnationals restructured their Canadian operations from servicing the domestic market to developing product mandates that served their continental or global production strategies. Continentalized production meant that these firms depended on virtually borderless production to stay profitable. In a corporate environment reconfigured by NAFTA to continentalize investment strategies, transnational business exerted pressure to ensure or safeguard free capital movements and the resulting trade flows.

In this economic review, we cannot omit the fact that the Bush administration pressed hard for a further integration of the three countries' energy sectors. Although the Canadian government was unlikely ever to say this out loud, it certainly had an energy card to play in negotiating some agreement on what kind of border controls were economically appropriate.

Neither could Mexico be excluded from this continental calculus. Fortress America would continue to need low-wage workers to do its menial work just as did its gated residential communities. Under globalized economic integration, "gringos" had to maintain a Third World inside their economy to stay competitive with real Third-World industrializers.

Yes, there were going to be new border burdens on business: tightened procedures; new surveillance technologies; advanced clearance of sealed trucks; high-tech ID for business travelers; placement of immigration and customs officials in each other's airports and seaports; and more detailed documentation describing the contents of shipments arriving from abroad. We may consider these changes to be the latest phase in managing a common frontier under conditions of advanced continentalization that have been adjusted to confront the new condition of sophisticated but containable terrorism. In short, it is NAFTA Minus.

Proponents of a deeper continental integration agenda seized the United States's catastrophe as an opportunity to shine their solutions for completing the job of continental union left unfinished by an imperfect NAFTA. A North American counterpart to the European Monetary Union—to be christened NAMU, perhaps—was a favorite candidate for those who saw Canada's future as a fully American territory, although Argentina's unhappy experience with dollarization made currency union without political influence a hard sell. A customs union whereby the three countries established a common external tariff would connect Canada and Mexico more closely to the American superstate. In neither case was much said about how the Americans would cope with Canadians and Mexicans having votes and seats on the Federal Reserve Board or having a say in determining how high their common tariffs should be. These developments might eventually see the light of day, but the post-catastrophe turmoil made a less-than-ideal midwife for their birthing. NAFTA Plus was a political nonstarter when those within Washington's beltway were focusing on Iraq.

Conclusion

The questions raised by September 11 about where the American perimeter would be drawn were far from answered a year and a half later because the associated issues were far from resolved:

- Militant Islam's terrorist capability remained unknown.
- Whether the Afghan war engendered a successful coalition of states, reinforced the world's hyperpower as global bully, or generated still more desperate ventures by the rogue states was undetermined.
- And for North America, one could not tell whether its integration would be deepened by a trilateral consensus on securing the continent against terrorism; whether the United States' borders would be raised so high that its two neighboring states would find themselves outside the fortress, with their NAFTA-accelerated vulnerability turned to their devastating disadvantage; or—more likely—whether the continent would

continue to be managed as two separate bilateral relationships by a hegemonic United States which refused any institution-alization that could diminish its freedom of maneuver.

We do know that the governments of Mexico and Canada strug-gled hard to be included within the United States' anti-terrorist defense zone. We know that the voices of business were heard loud and clear within the councils of all three governments, repeating a similar mes-sage. It is also clear that NAFTA itself had nothing to offer by way of institutions or processes that might insert themselves usefully in continental decisionmaking, as was proven by the absence of any tri-lateral summit to address these issues. So we can infer that the politics of post-catastrophe North America will see a reprise of the double dialogue of U.S.-Canada and U.S.-Mexico relations while perpetuat-ing an asymmetrical bilateralism that kept Washington comfortably in control. What Washington wanted would ultimately decide the main issues.

What Washington thought it wanted would be determined by a struggle of many forces. The final impact on Canada and the shape of North America would be directly affected by how prominently, loudly, and effectively the Canadian and Mexican governments inserted them-selves into this highly indeterminate situation. Any Ottawa battle for access to Washington's mind would need to activate moderate opin-ion leaders within the U.S. Success in this effort would likely depend on bringing to bear the skills the Canadian government had learned in wielding soft power within the United States, as when it negoti-ated a land mines treaty by mobilizing nongovernmental organizations around the world. Canadian diplomats have known for twenty-five years that there is no single recipe for managing the U.S. relationship because there is no single power center in the American system of government.

Canada was still living in 2003 under conditions of high indeter-minacy. Renewed terrorist attacks might foster an outcry across the continent for deeper political integration. A sustained exposure to ter-rorism might alternatively cause Americans to withdraw from both their northern and southern neighbors. NAFTA, for which so many working people laid down their jobs, had little to contribute toward furthering political integration. The border it was supposed to have erased might still become a barricade.

Notes

1. This chapter results from a series of presentations dealing with the significance of the events of September 11 for Canada. It benefited from the ensuing discussions during the past year at the Munk Centre for International Studies, University of Toronto; the Canadian Institute on International Affairs; the Canada-U.S. Fulbright program; the Walter Gordon Public Forum, the House of Commons Standing Committee on Foreign Affairs and International Trade; and, most germanely, the Watson Institute, Brown University, where this book was conceived. This text builds on earlier iterations of my ideas: "After the Catastrophe: Canada's Position in North America," *Behind the Headlines* 58, no. 3 (Spring 2001); "Lockstep in the Continental Ranks: Redrawing the American Perimeter after September 11," Canadian Centre for Policy Alternatives, February 2000; and "Strong and Free? Then Act That Way," *Globe and Mail,* June 20, 2002. Megan Merwart provided indispensable research assistance to give these texts more academic gravitas.
2. Paul Koring, "Bush Adds $2 Billion to Border Pot," *Globe and Mail,* January 26, 2002.
3. Daily two-way trade between Canada and the United States was at a level of Can. $1.91 billion (U.S. $1.28 billion) in 2000, and dipped to Can. $1.85 billion Canadian (U.S. $1.20 billion in 2001. See *Third Annual Report on Canada's State of Trade—Trade Update 2002,* May 2002, Department of Foreign Affairs and International Trade, www.dfait-maeci.gc.ca/eet/SOT_2002-e.pdf. Moreover, most Americans do not know that their economy's trade with Canada surpassed U.S. trade with all fifteen countries of the European Union. Even U.S. trade with the single province of Ontario exceeded American trade with Japan. See *Trade Update 2002,* www.dfait-maeci.gc.ca/eet/SOT_2002-e.pdf.
4. Department of Foreign Affairs and International Trade, "Canada Takes Defensive Action," *Canada World View* 14, (Winter 2002): 8.
5. Daniel Middlemiss and Denis Stairs, "The Canadian Forces and the Doctrine of Interoperability: The Issues," *Policy matters/Enjeux Publics* 37, June 2002. Institute for Research on Public Policy, 2002.
6. Interview at the Canadian embassy with Peter Boehm, April 11, 2002.
7. Shawn McCarthy, "Manley Defends Deployment," *Globe and Mail,* January 9, 2002, A4.
8. Paul Knox, "What Does the Canadian Military Have to Prove?," *Globe and Mail,* January 9, 2002, A9.
9. John Ibbitson and Shawn McCarthy, "Bush Apologizes to Canadians: 'I Wish We Could Bring Them Back'," *Globe and Mail,* April 20, 2002, A1; and John Ibbitson, "With a 'Friend' like This in the White House . . . ," *Globe and Mail,* May 6, 2002, A17.

10. J. L. Granatstein, "A Friendly Agreement in Advance: Canada-U.S. Defence Relations Past, Present, and Future," *C.D. Howe Institute Commentary: The Border Papers* 166 (June 2002).

11. Michael Byers, "On Guard for Uncle Sam?," *Globe and Mail*, April 14, 2002, A13.

12. Paul Knox, "The Risks of Collaboration," *Globe and Mail*, April 19, 2002, A15.

13. Jeff Sallot, "Canadian Soldiers Face Risks under U.S. Rule, Report Argues," *Globe and Mail*, April 26, 2002, A10.

14. Department of Foreign Affairs and International Trade, "Out of Horror Shine Decency and Goodness," *Canada World View* 14, (Winter 2002): 18–19.

15. During his visit to Ottawa in early December 2001, Attorney General John Ashcroft acknowledged it was Canadian intelligence that had enabled the FBI to apprehend the terrorist Ahmed Ressam when he crossed the British Columbia-Washington border in December 1999 intending to sabotage the Los Angeles airport.

16. "Preventing Illegal Migration and Efficiently Managing Legitimate Travel," www.canadianembassy.org/border/backgrounder-e.asp.

17. Graeme Smith, "Fictions Abound as U.S. Blames Canada," *Globe and Mail*, October 5, 2001.

18. Lawrence Martin, "We Didn't Mess up, They Did," *Globe and Mail*, December 18, 2001.

19. "Canada Takes Defensive Action," *Canada World View* 14 (Winter 2002): 7.

20. Ibid., 8.

21. Ibid., 6–7.

22. Bill C-11: Immigration and Refugee Protection Act Overview, www.cic.gc.ca/english/irpa/c1-overview.html.

23. Hugh Winsor, "Legislative Overkill? It's Hard to Tell," *Globe and Mail*, September 11, 2002, A7.

24. "Canada's Actions Against Terrorism Since September 11— Backgrounder," www.canadianembassy.org/border/backgrounder-e.asp.

25. "Action Plan for Creating a Secure and Smart Border," www.canam.gc.ca/ menu-e.asp?act=v&mid=1&cat=10&did=1248.

26. Shawn McCarthy, "Canada, U.S. Consider High-tech Preclearance," *Globe and Mail*, September 10, 2002, A8.

27. "Between Friends: The Canada-U.S. Connection," *Canada World View* 14 (Winter 2002): 9, 13.

28. Ginger Thompson, "After 9/11, Fox Still Waits for U.S. Moves on Mexico," *New York Times*, Sept. 13, 2002, A1, 14.

5

CANADA IN A NEW
NORTH AMERICA

LOUIS W. PAULY

Stephen Clarkson provides a capable overview of major developments in Canadian-American relations in the aftermath of 9-11. This chapter offers brief reflections on one of the principal questions raised by the editors of this book.[1] That question concerns how heightened perceptions of asymmetric economic and security interdependence after 9-11 are reshaping the political and policy landscape in Canada.[2] I contend that those perceptions have brought pragmatic policymakers to the fore, policymakers who are willing and able to make considerable compromises on border questions to retain as much room as possible to maneuver on the mainly domestic agenda of concern to their constituents. If 9-11 made many Americans think about the border in the black-and-white terms suggested by the phrase, "homeland security," their friends and allies to the north favored increasingly lighter shades of gray.

Personal Context

I cannot claim to be a disinterested observer of this process. The territorial boundary line between Canada and the United States runs straight down the middle of my family, and the psychological boundary has become more obvious to me over time. Born in the United States, I married a Canadian and have lived in the country for most of the past twenty-five years. Before coming here, I usually lived within thirty miles of the border, and my parents as well as brothers and sisters all still live within an one-hour drive of it. Before 9-11, we all crossed it routinely. Occasionally, customs and immigration officers on both sides would remind us that it involved a serious international frontier, most often when we traveled with a visitor whose citizenship was neither Canadian nor American. In recent years, all border-crossers had become painfully aware of the inadequacy of the physical bridges and the dramatic increase in traffic volume.

As for the psychological boundary, it has long seemed mainly a Canadian issue. Despite my location during my early life, just south of the forty-ninth parallel, I practically never thought about Canada. After moving north, the United States—its culture, society, economy, politics—has never been far from my thoughts. Before I took up residence here, Canada never influenced my life in any way that I can remember. Afterward, the United States—and Canadian reactions to U.S. influences—never ceased to have an impact on very many aspects of my life. My personal background and profession perhaps make me more aware of that impact, but certainly all of my relatives, friends, neighbors, and colleagues here in Canada could say the same thing. They often joke that the very core of Canadian identity is "not-American-ness." In truth, the punch line cannot sustain scrutiny.

Loyalist and so-called "late" Loyalist roots go deep in many extended Canadian families, including my own. The earlier ancestors were British-Americans, and the later ones were simply American citizens who moved north, mainly for economic reasons. French-Canadians, for their part, obviously descend from some of the earliest non-native settlers of North America. Their psychological relationship with the United States is more complicated, but its roots may be traced back to the Quebec Act passed by the British Parliament in 1774, which granted them considerable religious, cultural, and political autonomy in exchange for their neutrality in the coming British fight with their American colonies. The society built up over the following two centuries is notably distinctive. Confidence that it will remain so even in an integrating North American economy, combined with skillful strategic bargaining within the Canadian confederation, likely explains the fact that today Quebecers can be more pro-American than their counterparts in the rest of Canada. Finally, many newer Canadians have no such direct or historic connections to the United States; very few pay much attention to descendants of the Loyalists who still attend reenactments of scenes from the War of 1812 or to Quebecers who care about 1774. But they all routinely reflect on their current perceptions of the United States and redefine themselves in that changing light.

This is the psychological essence of the border matters that I want to highlight in this chapter. The awareness of power asymmetries in the Canadian-American relationship increased after 9-11, and that awareness was ever-present in the subsequent debate within Canada on the nature of the ideal border with its neighbor. As they had earlier in Canadian history, pragmatists won the debate almost as soon as it started. Practical efforts to narrow the power gap were never seriously contemplated. The objective was to save whatever could be saved of Canada's relative autonomy as a whole within an integrating North America. In substantial part, that meant revisiting and flexibly adjusting both the geographic and psychological borders with the United States.

In his seminal 1975 book on Canada's decision to take up arms in 1939, the Canadian historian Jack Granatstein described how World War II encouraged the development of Canadian nationalism and re-shaped Canada's perception of itself on the world stage. In going to war in its own right, and more than two years earlier than the United States, Granatstein contended, Canada "experienced a transition from semi-autonomous state to genuine nationhood."[3] From then until now, Canadian policymakers worked to define the terms of that nationhood, both internally and externally. This was never an easy matter, especially given a fundamental disagreement from the very beginning about the nature of "the people" comprising that "nation." Yet the external dimension that mainly concerns us here and the principal challenge remains what it has long been: to manage the complex and multifaceted relationship with an increasingly powerful and assertive American polity.

At the federal level, pragmatists most often have led the effort to meet that challenge. Occasionally, romantic visionaries have competed for the national soul. One of their visions idealized Canadian distinctiveness and promoted an ideology of social progessivism. In practical terms, they emphasized such objectives as maintaining a high-quality, publicly funded national health insurance system and promoting a high-profile (but low-cost) multilateralist and humanitarian foreign policy agenda. By the late 1980s, an ever-deepening experiment in continental economic integration, championed mainly by pragmatists, nevertheless trumped other externally oriented policies. Romantics may have hesitated as this course was pursued, but after September 11, 2001, both romantics and pragmatists became fully aware of the new trade-offs now existing between national autonomy and national security. The challenge was to recraft a set of policies that could define a new and stable midpoint between the fact of formal, legal sovereignty and the reality of intense economic, social, and military interdependence in a traumatized North America. The essence of the external dimension of that task was to reconstruct a physical and psychological border with the United States, one that would keep out as many problems as possible, while still allowing in as many opportunities as Canadians agreed were attractive. Neither high barriers nor open bridges would do. The new border had to be marked by a unique kind of fence. Once again, only pragmatists could plausibly promise to do the job. The widening continental asymmetry of power concentrated Canadian minds. The romantics were sidelined, and the pragmatists returned to the forefront of national policymaking.

Contemplating the Border in the Modern Era

If one lumped the disparate Canadian population together, the vast majority would surely locate themselves in the middle of a political spectrum extending from the moderate left to the moderate right.[4] I am personally acquainted with colleagues and students who inhabit the fringes of that admittedly limited spectrum. On the basis of this personal knowledge, I concluded before September 11, 2001 that those at both political extremes agreed on at least one thing: that when I moved here in the late 1970s, I had caught the tail end of the country's brief experience as a proud, independent, and unique state. That experience, according to those colleagues and students who perhaps agree on little else, began in earnest when the British Empire started unraveling after World War I; it gathered serious momentum during World War II, and it reached its apogee in a vast national exposition held in Montreal in 1967. On the moderate left, the euphoria of postcolonial patriotism, new beginnings, national distinctiveness marked especially by bilingualism, multiculturalism, and a commitment to building a

European-style social democracy soon dissipated.[5] From a moderate right point-of-view, not dissimilarly, it is commonly held that the energy symbolized by Expo '67 was almost immediately squandered.[6] In fact, right across the political spectrum, it has not been unusual in recent years to hear Canadians opine that an independent and secure nation entered its twilight period when a combination of internal financial and industrial mismanagement, enervating battles over separatism in Quebec, and a series of bilateral and multilateral trade and investment agreements seriously eroded the internal capacity decisively to influence the terms of engagement with the wider world, and especially with the United States.

In the aftermath of 9-11, the sense of anxiety shared by adherents of such a view deepened. For my less sanguine acquaintances on the moderate left, the likely scenario after 9-11 was a sad but seemingly inexorable drift back to colonial status, but this time with the imperial center now shifted from London to Washington. As for those on the moderate right, they cannot yet seem to articulate a preferable outcome, but the logic of their position suggests political and social union with the United States, albeit as a very junior member of that union.

The sense of foreboding, it seems, is now widely shared. A respected public opinion poll conducted nearly a year after 9-11 found that 30 percent of Canadians believe that an independent Canada will not exist in twenty-five years, while 42 percent believe that it "probably" will. The fact that this is not a happy prospect for most is implied in the answer of the same respondents to the question of whether political and economic integration across North America, perhaps modeled on the experiment underway in contemporary Europe, is desirable. Nearly 60 percent said "no."[7] After 9-11, Canadians were groping for some alternative future. But the basic challenge they faced was not new.

In 1867, the fathers of Canadian Confederation decided to do whatever they could to stop a North American political union from emerging in the aftermath of the American Civil War—a war, by the way, in which thousands of Canadians fought on the Union side. After 1945, and more recently after Expo '67, their successors aspired to build a Canada distinct from the United States but not antagonistic to it. Long after the British connection had become mainly sentimental, all Canadians appeared to want a high degree of policy autonomy *and* a level of prosperity reasonably close to the average in the United States. Many seemed also to favor the construction and maintenance of a fairer, cleaner, and safer society than the one they perceived to exist to the south. To achieve such objectives, the more practical minds among them knew that the country needed a novel kind of border with the United States.

Physically, that border would have to continue, as it historically had, to restrict the inflow of many kinds of problems (to be blunt, problems associated with poor people, with guns, drugs, disease, and cultural influences unwanted by the national elite). It would have to be designed in such a way as not to impede the inward flow of the people, money, goods, and ideas deemed desirable by most Canadians. In addition, such a border would have to accommodate certain kinds of outflows, not just of prosperity-creating exports and investments, but also of people. Some of those people—like students, skilled workers, and "snowbirds" seeking warmer weather in the winter—might eventually return home, but others would find opportunities in the United States that they could not find in Canada. Certain pressures potentially disruptive of the social and political balance would thereby find a release; the border would provide a helpful sort of safety valve. Very important, the ideal physical border would also have to be porous enough to allow Canadians to benefit from American military preparedness and for good policy ideas and artistic creations occasionally to filter out of Canada into the right American circles. But it would have to be not so porous as to render vacuous the historical claim of Canadians to legal sovereignty over a given territory.[8]

That unique kind of border had to have an irreducible psychological dimension. For example, it could not be like the border between New York and Pennsylvania after the Civil War and the emergence of industrial capitalism. The difference between those two kinds of borders had to be sufficient to ground a sense of national identity robust enough for Canadians to sustain a modern state of their own. Richard Gwyn evocatively called this a sense of "nationalism without walls," but it might be more accurate to call it nationalism behind a well-constructed kind of fence.[9]

Such a fence had analogs elsewhere. Something like it surely signified the core of the new international political and economic system that the United States, Great Britain, and Canada did so much to design in the mid-1940s. Our leading international relations textbooks still use the word "interdependence" to suggest the essence of that system, a term that implies a half-way point between intimate political union and extreme fragmentation. In practice, the post-1967 Canadian fence gradually evolved in such a way as to suggest more than interdependence. By September 10, 2001, it actually evoked another half-way point—this one somewhere between full union and symmetrical interdependence. The fence at the border marked a shifting line between economic, social, and military integration and cultural and political autonomy.

In the wake of their World War II alliance and joint efforts during the Cold War, Canadians had long ago willingly locked themselves into U.S.-led security arrangements within North America. In the wake of the Canada-U.S. Free Trade Agreement and the subsequent North American Free Trade Agreement, the Canadian economy was ever more deeply integrated into a U.S.-centered continental economy. In neither case did this imply the irrevocable loss of formal legal integrity or the necessity of political union. Canadians retained all the modern trappings of independent citizenship. Many Canadians, however, did not really view themselves as "foreigners" in the still separate American political system. The owners of second homes in the American Sun Belt; students studying on a full- or part-time basis south of the border; dual nationals; employees of American companies and of companies entirely dependent on sales to the U.S. market; and families with close American relatives and friends surely comprise the majority of the contemporary Canadian population. Notwithstanding the old joke about Canadian identity, to be Canadian today cannot be "to be not-American." If there remains a constituency for radical separateness from the United States, it has little political significance. But there remains a large constituency for maintaining a geographic and psychological buffer between Canada and the United States—*if* it can be achieved at reasonable economic and political cost. To assess the continuing Canadian debate over the nature of the post–9-11 border, it is important to understand the complicated but entirely rational balancing of interests required to satisfy just such a constituency.

The Contemporary Challenge

Even before September 11, 2001, it was clear that the generation of 1967 had failed to build and maintain a country as prosperous as the United States. The general standard of living in Canada was lower, productivity increases had not kept pace, and the quality of many public services, health, and social security systems had obviously declined over a twenty-year period.[10] Moreover, the quality of the physical environment had deteriorated in obvious and non-obvious ways.[11] With homelessness growing in its major cities, even staunch nationalists began to question whether their society was really fairer or more equitable than the one to the south.

The vision glimpsed at Expo '67 had dissipated by the late 1990s, but what remained could hardly be characterized in terms of hopelessness or despair. Nearly 30,000,000 people continued to reside in what, for most, remained a very desirable place, and there was no shortage of highly skilled workers seeking entry. To be sure, some Canadians, especially descendants of aboriginal groups, continued to live in abysmal conditions. But by global standards, most Canadians remained very lucky and they knew it. The events of 9-11 nevertheless shocked them into confronting the potentially ephemeral nature of that good fortune. Their subsequent perceptions, and policy reactions based on those perceptions, remained unsettled throughout the following year and into the next. There were, and are, many things to consider. But soon after 9-11, Canadians could not avoid addressing urgent questions concerning practical border arrangements with the United States.

An excellent scholarly review of Canadian politics and policy is published annually in a series called *Canada Among Nations*. The edition published in 2000 bore the retrospectively ironic subtitle, *Vanishing Borders*.[12] In the aftermath of 9-11, the wielders of serious political power in Canada were forced to focus their undivided attention on borders that clearly were not vanishing. They were mainly located around the shifting center of the governing Liberal Party. The Liberals had long been viewed as the natural governing party at the federal level, and they now controled a government virtually indistinguishable from the Party itself. As in the case of the Liberal Democrats in Japan, the fact of long periods in power never implied the emergence of a fully coherent policy agenda.[13] There remained intense personal and ideological rivalries within the Party. Indeed, one longstanding personal struggle for supremacy between Prime Minister Jean Chrétien and Finance Minister Paul Martin dramatically intensified after 9-11, during the spring of 2002, when Martin left the Cabinet and began a public campaign for Party leadership. By late summer, Chrétien announced that he would not run in a fourth election as head of the Liberals and that he would resign the prime ministership in February 2004. Future historians may or may not tell us that 9-11 was decisive in fundamentally recasting governing arrangements in Canada. What we can already begin to assess is the impact 9-11 had on a deeper division within the Liberal Party, which arguably reflected a similar split among the great majority of the country's citizenry.

I focus the balance of this chapter on how that division initially played out on the question of the border. In this regard, the terms "left" and "right" are inadequate. "Romantic" and "pragmatic" as used above are not much better, but they do suggest an important difference in emphasis in a continuing debate over the best means for shaping and harnessing a sense of nationalism to provide a foundation for coherent policies. If we developed an analytical framework to contrast the idealism of what we might call the romantic wing of the Liberal Party with the realism of the pragmatic wing, the essential post–9-11 story is about the rising fortunes in the latter camp. The contest was symbolized within the federal cabinet but it resonated more broadly. At its heart was the matter of the border, specifically of the unique kind of border Canadians had painstakingly tried to construct during the decades extending back to 1945, and perhaps even earlier.

Inside the Party, 9-11 profoundly deepened a debate that had really commenced in earnest in 1994. Between 1984 and 1993, the Conservative Party under Prime Minister Brian Mulroney had managed to dislodge the ruling Liberals. With their most significant support coming from Quebec and the western provinces, the Conservatives set an ambitious agenda for themselves. They wanted to accommodate Quebec's demands for greater autonomy under new constitutional arrangements, to bring the country's deteriorating financial condition under control, and to enhance Canada's overall security in a turbulent world. The latter goal entailed matching the existing degree of military and intelligence integration with the United States, signified especially by the joint North American Aerospace Defense Command (NORAD), with new economic arrangements promising preferential Canadian access to American markets. Only on the last item did they eventually record significant new progress. The Canada-U.S. Free Trade Agreement of 1988 (in effect 1989), followed in 1992 by the North American Free Trade Agreement (in effect 1994), was to be their principal legacy.[14] For their efforts and their failures, the election of December 1993 revealed that their more immediate legacy was to be the destruction of their own political base. From then on, the Conservatives themselves struggled to retain a handful of seats in Parliament and they bequeathed to the Liberals the gift of a deeply fractured opposition.

The Liberals came back to power vowing comprehensive change. With a bit of luck, but only after nearly losing yet another referendum on Quebec's separation, they had more success on the unity issue. They also, and quite remarkably, succeeded in turning the national fiscal situation around. Despite some campaign rhetoric to the contrary, once back in office they decided not to back away from either military or economic integration with the United States. Some among the Liberals certainly minded the military imbalance at times; it bothered them, for example, that American submarines had free and unimpeded access to northern Canadian territorial waters. But most of the caucus, like most of their constituents, apparently found the status quo quite acceptable. As for moving away from the booming U.S. market for Canadian exports (now over 80 percent of total exports), from open financial markets for Canadian investors and borrowers, and from an attractive job market for mobile Canadians, Liberal support for actually reversing associated Conservative policies quickly dwindled. With just-in-time delivery systems working reasonably well across national frontiers (especially in an automotive sector that comprised nearly half of Ontario's economy); with rapidly expanding cross-border mobility of capital and certain kinds of people; with information, ideas, and entertainment crossing the forty-ninth parallel at the fastest possible speed Intel, Microsoft, CNN, and Disney could provide; and with the country engaged in high-profile, but not too onerous peacekeeping missions around the world, a new Canadian identity seemed on the horizon. Some called it postnational, others postmodern. In its shadow, the Liberals managed three decisive victories in back-to-back federal elections. Happy days were soon to be here again, or at least that is how it looked before September 11, 2001.

Romantics within the party once again were becoming more visible. The industry minister was calling for a new innovation agenda, which implied old-style economic intervention to save indigenous firms and kick-start new ones. The culture minister talked confidently about new policies to promote and sustain vehicles for Canadians to refine a new identity freed from the pressures of competing head-on with New York and Hollywood (even while attracting investments from Hollywood studios in a burgeoning Canadian film industry). The foreign minister railed against American dominance and struggled mightily to create a distinctive and progressive role for Canada on the world stage, a role identified mainly with peacekeeping, an international criminal court, and a convention on landmines. After three elections, Liberal romantics began to sense an opportunity for rekindling the spirit of 1967. It is true that Liberal pragmatists began trimming the sails of their romantic brethren just before 9-11. Foreign Minister Lloyd Axworthy, for example, had recently been forced out, and Paul Martin's continuing budgetary stringency had effectively derailed the more ambitious plans coming from the industry and culture ministries. But the events of 9-11 did more than anything to vitiate a romantic policy line.

On the day of the disaster itself and immediately afterward, the prime minster demonstrated a characteristic measure of caution. The people of Canada were quicker and the general reaction was one of solidarity with the Americans at a time of great tragedy. When American authorities closed their airspace, Canada immediately provided landing spots for all inbound aircraft. Local communities around the country did whatever they could to help, and they did so spontaneously. They welcomed stranded air travelers, donated blood, volunteered their medical and construction skills, and sent financial aid. For its part, the Canadian military was engaged in support operations from the start, under the umbrella of NORAD and other longstanding bilateral defense agreements.[15] Canadian officers were in NORAD's

Cheyenne Mountain command center and were completely engaged in integrated operations.

Canadian government officials and the general population sincerely shared the pain Americans felt on 9-11, and not just because some two dozen Canadians had died in the World Trade Center. In the days that followed, their emotions nevertheless mixed with shock at the consequences for Canada of draconian American reactions to the tragedy. Central to their realization of those consequences were developments at the border. On 9-11, it was effectively closed—just like that. When it opened again, it did so under a drastically more rigorous inspection regime. With trade flows now averaging U.S. $1.3 billion daily, and some 200 million personal trips across the border logged annually, the costs mounted rapidly. The long lines of trucks stuck behind the border bridges had ominous implications for the post-NAFTA economy, around which vital national interests now revolved.

Immediately following 9-11, pragmatists in the federal government moved front and center. John Manley, who had recently taken over as foreign minister, took the lead role in reassuring Americans—without conditions—that Canada could be trusted. The full story of what happened next has yet to be told. When it is, it will likely show that Manley's department, together with the Department of National Defence, the Royal Canadian Mounted Police, the Canadian Security and Intelligence Service, and the Finance Department, moved amazingly swiftly and effectively to craft a strategy designed to convince the Americans that their northern frontier was absolutely secure. New anti-terrorism legislation was passed in Parliament with unusual speed. Immigration regulations were tightened. Not simply to bring the message home, even if it did have that effect, Canadian military units—long since adapted for peacekeeping tasks—were sent directly into combat in Afghanistan. (They were apparently deployed at Canada's request and not following an American invitation.) In short, the government moved with exceptional speed to reassure the United States and ultimately to get ahead of the developing bilateral policy curve on border matters.

The strategy of reassurance took a while to succeed, perhaps because of understandable disarray on the American side in the immediate aftermath of 9-11. Over the next few months, despite the eventual success of Canada's pragmatism, new American policies continued to present awkward problems, most of which were countered with new Canadian initiatives to carve out special exceptions. For example, American immigration rules now specified that foreigners could only spend 30 days in the country. Did that mean Canadians too? Yes, came the initial reply. Yet within days, and surely after a few hurried telephone calls to senators from Florida and Arizona by or on behalf of the Canadian Association of Retired People, the American czar for Homeland Security, Tom Ridge, and now-Deputy Prime Minister John Manley hammered out a deal exempting Canadians. Similar negotiations ensued when Ontario students studying on a part-time basis in Buffalo, especially in nursing programs, found themselves ensnared by new regulations presumably aimed mainly at curtailing foreign enrollment in American flight-training schools. In managing such challenges, multilateralism was fine in theory, but there proved to be no substitute for pragmatic bilateralism in practice. By the late summer of 2002, negotiations along these lines had culminated in new arrangements, among other things, to create fast lanes at key border points for precleared and low-risk transport vehicles and frequent travelers.[16] With regard to military cooperation, new agreements effectively linked Canadian Forces to the new U.S. Northern Command; in operational terms, one dimension involved the establishment of a binational committee empowered to declare the existence of continental crises that could automatically trigger the deployment of American troops to Canada and of Canadian troops to the United States.[17]

In the difficult months following 9-11, Canadian policymakers moved skillfully and quickly to save whatever could be saved of a geographic and psychological border that might continue to meet traditional Canadian objectives. The clear and present danger was that the border would once again become a serious barrier to post-NAFTA national aspirations. Those aspirations were rooted in the earlier history discussed briefly above, but now they surely concentrated on the following: to preserve some policy autonomy on a full range of issues—but not too much; to continue cooperating on continental defense (without requiring massive increases in defense spending, without turning Canada into a surrogate target for the enemies of the United States, and without compromising Canada's ultimate legal sovereignty); to keep some distance from perceived excesses of U.S. social, political, and economic organization; and to approximate U.S. levels of economic prosperity without completely abandoning the ideal of social equity.[18]

Romantics within the Liberal Party and elsewhere did not disappear, and the prime minister knew how to move them. But after 9-11, their alternative agenda became vague and grounded more on hopes than clear policy ideas. Their general stance could be interpreted as anti-American, but it would be more accurate to say that they were engaged in a rear-guard action to preserve some sense of meaningful distinctiveness from the United States. Against the odds, but still resonating with now-repressed stirrings deep in the national polity, they forced their constituents to reflect on the potential long-term consequences of the regional power asymmetries that the events of 9-11 had unmasked.

In any event, a desire to retain power within Canada continued most of the time to unite romantics and pragmatists within the governing coalition. In this regard it may be argued plausibly that the more extreme conservative views emanating from official Washington strengthened cohesion within the Liberal Party. Indeed, one year after 9-11, Canadians as a whole seemed increasingly focused on the objective of rebuilding sufficiently effective organs of national governance. By this, I mean a reasonably well-functioning state capable of defending interests broadly viewed as truly vital. The public opinion poll cited earlier indicates what this means in practice and the order in which Canadians rank those interests.

The term "sovereignty" is commonly used to suggest effective power and intuitively seems to be required to preserve and promote national values and interests. When asked what things they valued that would require sovereignty to be preserved in this sense, 83 percent of Canadians surveyed listed the country's natural resources, 81 percent the national health system, 66 percent the economy, 64 percent immigration, 61 percent national defense, 58 percent the currency, 52 percent the system of transfer payments across the provinces (known as equalization), and 49 percent arts and culture.[19] It is doubtful that Americans would respond the same way, but a logical follow-on question for Canadians might concern the nature of the border that their list of priorities would imply. The answer is surely too complicated for a straightforward survey of opinions, and the question was not asked. Yet we can infer one from Canadian policy during the year after September 11, 2001.

Despite the fears of economic nationalists, freer trade has been popular in Canada and its benefits are widely recognized. The kind of border that facilitates trade and investment is precisely what was lost in the initial period after 9-11; government at both national and provincial levels accordingly devoted considerable time and energy to restoring it. Moreover, high-profile trade disputes with the United States, for example, on softwood lumber, combined with enthusiasm for the freer movement of goods, services, and investment, increased prominent calls after 9-11 for moving beyond NAFTA toward a customs union with the United States.[20] As long as further economic integration stops short of monetary union, for which little enthusiasm is apparent in the country, the cause is likely to increase in popularity. In any case, virtually no serious constituency exists to turn back the clock by rendering the trade and investment aspect of the border less porous.[21]

On the issue of further military integration across the border, Liberal pragmatists, reflective of public opinion, are only slightly more circumspect. The reasons are formal and financial. Significant increases in military spending are not popular, certainly not when health care, social security, and education systems are generally perceived to require new investments. There is good reason why Canadians do not see themselves as directly threatened by foreign adversaries. With troop strength at 14,000, the truth is that they have nearly disarmed. This could help to explain why the idea that American soldiers will, under crisis conditions, now be freely deployed north of the forty-ninth parallel was not immediately met with loud opposition. To the contrary, although most Canadians would rank them low on their list of priorities, decisions to increase the interoperability of American and Canadian forces, such as they are, and even to increase military spending to the minimum level required to satisfy moderate American demands, appear to be on the immediate horizon. It would even be reasonable to predict that serious controversy on these matters will be limited mainly to the environs of universities. In short, the idea that Canadians should support their main ally—even if grudgingly when the threat is abstract—is popular, as is the notion that Americans will come to Canada's aid in the unlikely event that it comes under attack. If I am right, this means that the majority of Canadians actually desire the kind of border that such military cooperation requires.

On the other hand, the border of the future that Canadians desire will still be robust enough to filter immigrants, to stop the unrestricted sale of certain natural resources—especially fresh water, to curtail access to subsidized health care by non-Canadians, to limit the flow of personal firearms, and to prevent foreign investments in related spheres from undermining the public character of the health care system. After 9-11, Canadians, led by Liberal pragmatists, demonstrated a clear commitment to reconstructing just the right kind of border with the United States. By the end of 2002, they seemed close to realizing it.

As in earlier times in Canadian history, that right kind of border reemerges as central to the continuing challenge of holding a big, fractious country together. Romantics have never shown themselves capable of meeting that challenge. Nor have cynics. The fact that border issues became unsettled in the wake of 9-11 explains why pragmatists within government remain front and, of course, center. There is nothing disreputable in this. When push comes to shove, Canadians as a collectivity show themselves repeatedly to be capable of acting strategically. They understand the forces they are up against. If it is true that over 70 percent of them have doubts about the durability of their political arrangements in a new North America, it remains true that they know how to hedge their bets. They recognize opportunities when they see them and they distrust grand ideologies. They know what they want at the moment and they are prepared to compromise to achieve it.

Conclusion

The majority of Canadians proved in the immediate aftermath of September 11 that they perceived their principal interests on vital questions of world order to be identical with their cousins to the south. As already noted, many had the chance to demonstrate this when they welcomed those planes diverted from American airspace, when they converged on Parliament Hill and elsewhere for large and sincere memorial services, and when they rallied behind the American-led war in Afghanistan, even at the tragic cost of the lives of Canadian soldiers. They accept the necessity of greatly enhanced cooperation between Canadian and American military forces. They continue to favor freer trade, freer investment, and freer mobility for at least some kinds of labor. They also continue to be appalled by the consequences of social inequities in the United States (like the absence of health insurance for 40 million Americans), consequences that, they fully understand, potentially can travel northward. They fear a stark, strong border that can impede desired two-way flows of resources. But they also fear a too-weak border that cannot impede various kinds of undesired flows. To avoid both potential developments, they are quite willing to accommodate U.S. concerns; again, by and large, they share most of those concerns intimately. Yet the vast majority has not given up the hope that they can simultaneously rebuild both the right kind of border and their own kind of state—minimally, one capable of managing that border in their own interest. These are the people whom pragmatic policymakers within the governing Liberal Party are trying to hold. But what if they cannot hold them?

The two extreme sides of the spectrum of possibilities are imaginable, if only dimly in the wake of some further and even more appalling tragedy than that of 9-11. On one side, a far right-of-center coalition could come to power and complete the task of cross-border integration, with all of the attendant social and political disruption this would entail for both Canada and the Unites States. On the other side, a coalition led by romantics of the left could come to power, borne on an emotional wave of anti-Americanism but inevitably proving itself capable only of leading to a system benefiting an elite few Canadians.

A safer bet, supported by most of Canada's history since 1867 and certainly since 1945, is that pragmatists will hold on to power. A worthwhile hope is that they can use that power to finally move beyond a minimal and mainly defensive national project. Such a project cannot really be anti-American. To the extent that the vision of 1967 depended on an identity molded by any such sense, it was always doomed. I am not the first to point out that Canadians undeniably *are* Americans.

They are, however, Americans whose history has led them in their own ways not to fully embrace United Statesianism. The specific task for the next generation of Canadian pragmatists could be to actually build a better America north of the forty-ninth parallel.

Nothing bothers Canadians more than to be labeled free riders and, in the aftermath of 9-11, such an accusation was once again borne aloft by fears on both sides of the border. Rebutting it, while also attempting to recover the pre–9-11 status quo, can explain much about contemporary Canadian policies. To the extent the United States agrees with those policies—like those conducive to more fluid border traffic and greater military cooperation—perhaps it would be best if American policymakers would strive to remember ancient truths about the dangers of hubris, the necessity of leavening power with wisdom, and the impossibility of constructing a new sense of authority, either on a continental or a global basis, on a foundation of resentment. I would even go so far as to say that anti-Americanism, to the extent it does exist in Canada, needs to be stoked from outside, for example, by loud demands for policy convergence and for conformity with laws and customs over which outsiders have no leverage. In an open and increasingly complex society, the kind of border Canadians want and need poses no challenge to the United States that cannot be addressed with skillful, low-level diplomacy. The editor-in-chief of the country's leading newspaper puts it like this: "We're willing to grow closer economically if that's what it takes to ensure prosperity. But don't ask us to give up those things that truly give us meaning as a people."[22]

For the foreseeable future, the underlying objective of contemporary Canadian pragmatists will be the same as the one orienting the constitutive policies of their predecessors. As a friend of mine put it in the title of a wonderful little book, that objective is to remain "as Canadian as possible, under the circumstances."[23] In practice, once again, that means reconstructing the right kind of border. The image of a flexible form of fencing with many types of gates seems apt. In the end, however, work on the geographic and psychological boundary line between Canada and the United States entails the much more complicated matter of reconceiving and reconstituting compatible, stable, and prosperous political communities—ones open to each other, but still as autonomous as it is feasible to be. Ultimately, this calls for reciprocal action among wise leaders and willing followers. Even after 9-11, there is no necessary reason why such wisdom or such will should be in short supply.

Notes

1. For comments on an earlier draft, I am grateful to the editors and the participants in the February 2002 conference held at Brown University; for research assistance, I thank Marc Kosciejew and the Social Sciences and Humanities Research Council of Canada.
2. For the beginnings of what later became a voluminous body of research on asymmetrical interdependence, specifically including the case of Canada, see Robert O. Keohane and Joseph Nye, *Power and Interdependence* (Boston: Little, Brown, 1977).
3. J.L. Granatstein, *Canada's War: The Politics of the Mackenzie King Government, 1939–1945* (Toronto: University of Toronto Press, 1975).
4. As one of my senior colleagues asks his students every year, "Why did the Canadian cross the road?" The correct response: "To get to the middle."
5. For a recent analysis, see Stephen Clarkson, *Uncle Sam and Us* (Toronto: University of Toronto Press, 2002).
6. Michael Bliss, "Is Canada a Country in Decline?" *National Post* (November 30, 2001), commentary section.
7. *Maclean's-L'actualite* (CROP) poll, *Maclean's Magazine* (September 9, 2002): 38. For an attempt to tease subtle, and perhaps more acceptable, analogies out of the European case, see Robert A. Pastor, *Toward a North American Community* (Washington, D.C.: Institute for International Economics, 2001).
8. For historical background, see John English and Norman Hillmer (eds.), *Making a Difference? Canada's Foreign Policy in a Changing World Order* (Toronto: Lester Publishing, 1992).
9. Richard Gwyn, *Nationalism Without Walls: The Unbearable Lightness of Being Canadian* (Toronto: McClelland and Stewart, 1997).
10. In 2001, GDP per Canadian worker was close to 80 percent of the American comparator, while after-tax income stood at 69 percent. Labor productivity was 81 percent of the U.S. equivalent. Data compiled by the Centre for the Study of Living Standards. See www.csls.ca.
11. See Sierra Club of Canada, "Rio + 10: The Tenth Annual Report Card," www.sierraclub.ca.
12. Maureen Appel Molot and Fen Osler Hampson, eds., *Canada Among Nations 2000: Vanishing Borders* (Toronto: Oxford University Press, 2000).
13. For essential background, see Christina McCall, *Grits: An Intimate Portarit of the Liberal Party* (Toronto: Macmillan of Canada, 1982).
14. On the latter agreement, see Maxwell A. Cameron and Brian W. Tomlin, *The Making of NAFTA* (Ithaca, N.Y.: Cornell University, 2000).
15. For details, see www.dnd.ca and www.defenselink.mil/news/April2002.

16. *New York Times,* September 10, 2002, A1. The acronym was FAST, for the Free and Secure Trade Program. The speedier movement of people was to be assured through a new system for frequent travelers called NEXUS.

17. *New York Times,* August 15, 2002, A11.

18. The latter objective was central to a long and continuing debate on how to counteract the effects of a "brain drain" to the United States that was principally limited to medical services, high-technology and knowledge-intensive industries, and parts of academia. See Statistics Canada, "Brain Drain and Brain Gain: The Migration of Knowledge Workers From and To Canada," *Education Quarterly Review* 6 (May 2000): 8–35.

19. *Maclean's-L'actualite* (CROP) poll, *Maclean's Magazine* (September 9, 2002): 38. Quebecers were notably less enthusiastic to preserve sovereignty across every category except equalization payments (56 percent) and arts and culture (50 percent).

20. See, for example, Allan Gotlieb, "Why not a grand bargain with the U.S.?" *National Post,* September 11, 2002, commentary section.

21. No contradiction is implied to the findings of John Helliwell about the still-enduring effects of the border itself on the intensity of interprovincial economic linkages. See Helliwell, *How Much Do Borders Matter?* (Washington, D.C.: The Brookings Institution, 1998).

22. Edward Greenspon, "Building the New Canadian," *The Globe and Mail,* November 10, 2001, F4.

23. Linda Hutcheon, *As Canadian as Possible, Under the Circumstances* (Toronto: ECW Press and York University, 1990).

6

THE FALSE CONUNDRUM

Continental Integration versus Homeland Security

STEPHEN E. FLYNN[1]

North America finds itself in paradoxical times. On the one hand, the continent's economic prosperity depends on an open global system that facilitates the free movement of people and goods. On the other, worries over America's exposure to catastrophic terrorist attacks have transformed homeland security into Washington's leading preoccupation. Consequently, there is a potential train wreck in the making. Moving in one direction are those who have been keen to make national borders as porous as possible so as to spawn greater economic integration. From the other are anxious U.S. politicians who look to the border to hold back would-be terrorists, contraband, criminals, and illegal migrants.

Now that the attacks of September 11 have let the catastrophic terrorist genie out of the bottle, the United States has legitimate cause to be nervous about its security at home. This new sobriety arises from three realities that flow from the catbird position that the United States occupies as the world's sole superpower. First, since no U.S. adversary can realistically aspire to victory on the field of battle by going toe-to-toe with conventional U.S. military forces, they must avail themselves of the asymmetric tactics of David seeking to topple Goliath. Second, in addition to its military muscle, America's economic and cultural dominance means that it will continue to generate hostility among those who find its supremacy objectionable. Last, the open nature of U.S. society along with the sophisticated, concentrated, and interdependent critical infrastructures that support its way of life make it a "target-rich" environment for catastrophic terrorist attacks.

Yet, however compelling the homeland security imperative may be, it should not mean a derailment of the continental engine of free trade and travel. U.S. prosperity—and much of its power—relies on its ready access to North American and global networks of transport, energy, information, finance, and labor. It is self-defeating for the United States to embrace security measures that isolate it from those networks. In addition, there is little value to singularly focusing on bolstering the defenses of only those parts of networks that lie within U.S. jurisdiction. Such an approach is like building a firewall only around the computer server physically nearest to a network security manager while leaving the remaining remote servers unprotected.

Further, the experience over the past decade of stepped-up enforcement along the Mexican border suggests that U.S. efforts aimed at hardening its borders can have the unintended consequence of creating precisely the kind of environment that is conducive to terrorists and criminals. On the face of it, an emphasis on tighter border controls appears logical. Stopping threats at the frontier is better than trying to cope with them once inside the country. Customs inspectors and immigration officials also have the strongest legal authority for inspecting and searching people and goods. But draconian measures to police the border invariably provide incentives for informal arrangements and criminal conspiracies to overcome cross-border barriers to commerce and labor movements. In addition, unilateral measures pursued on one side of the border create political impediments for enforcement cooperation on the other. As a result, the border region becomes more chaotic and thus ideal for exploitation by criminals and terrorists.

The alternative is to look beyond national borders as a line of defense. Terrorists and the tools of terrorism do not spring up at the border. Instead, they generally arrive via hemispheric and international trade and travel networks. Advancing a continental approach to deterring, detecting, and intercepting illicit actors seeking to exploit those networks would accomplish two things. First, it would provide strategic depth for responding to a threat before it arrived at a critical and congested border crossing; second, it would mean the ability to segment risk and facilitate the cross-border movements of people and cargo deemed a low-risk. Then limited enforcement resources could be more effectively targeted at those that present a high risk.

The twenty-first century imperatives that fuel both the incentives for advancing hemispheric economic integration and satisfying the new homeland security mandate do not inevitably involve trade-offs. On the contrary, the shared risks of loss of life and massive economic disruption presented by the catastrophic terrorist threat should provide the basis for trilateral cooperation, which can remove many longstanding barriers to continental commerce precisely because those barriers themselves can elevate security risks. For example, the longstanding neglect of the border in terms of limited infrastructure investment and tepid efforts at customs and immigration modernization and harmonization made no sense in purely economic terms. But the resultant inefficiencies that carry substantial commercial costs also create opportunities that thugs and terrorists can exploit. Thus, there is a national security rationale to redress those inefficiencies. The agendas for both promoting security and greater continental commerce can be and must be mutually reinforcing.

The Hardened Border Paradox

Great powers have been building great walls throughout history. The Great Wall of China, the Maginot Line, and the Berlin Wall went up at considerable expense in sweat and treasure, and all ultimately failed to block or contain the forces that prompted their construction. The recent efforts by the United States to "protect" the southwest border, including installing a 26-mile long fence between San Diego and Tijuana, has had a similar fate.

Take the case of illegal migration. Stepped-up patrolling and policing of the border may raise the costs of getting to the United States, but it also creates a demand for those who are in the business of arranging the illegal crossings. Migrants who once simply strolled across the border to seek work on the other side, now need "professional" help. That help is provided by guides known as "coyotes" who take migrants to remote border locations or put together increasingly sophisticated smuggling operations at the land border entries. As the coyote business becomes more lucrative, criminal gangs are better positioned to invest in pay-offs of front-line agents.[2] The prevalence of corruption, in turn, undermines information sharing and operational coordination between U.S. authorities and their Mexican counterparts.

Enforcement-driven delays at the border also ironically contribute to creating opportunities for smuggling narcotics. In Laredo, Texas, for instance, truck crossings were at 2.8 million in 1999, up from 1.3 million in 1993.[3] Many of these trucks operating at the border are old and poorly maintained and are owned by small mom-and-pop trucking companies. The turnover rate among drivers is extremely high because they wait hours at a border crossing to make a 20–mile round trip, and with an empty trailer on the return trip, it is not a lucrative business for the owners. Moving intercontinental freight is, so the trucks and drivers who make long-haul journeys tend to be of a higher quality. Since it is uneconomical to run a state-of-the-art rig near the border, trailers are usually offloaded at depots near the border. In the case of south-bound traffic, an expediter will contract a short-haul truck to move the freight to a customs broker who will then order another short-haul truck to transport the freight to another depot across the border. A long-haul truck will then pick up the load and carry it into the interior. The drivers of these short-haul rigs tend to be younger, less skilled, and are paid only nominal wages—as little as $7 to $10 per trip. As a result, the potential payoff for carrying contraband through a congested border crossing is all the more tempting.[4]

The White House Office of National Drug Control Policy estimates that more than half of the cocaine that arrives in the United States comes across the southwest border.[5] Even with the rise in the number of inspectors and investigators assigned to the 28 border-entry points in Texas, New Mexico, Arizona, and California, and given both the volume and the nature of the trucking sector that services the border, the U.S. government clearly faces "needle-in-a-haystack" odds as it strives to detect and intercept illicit drugs. The pure cocaine to feed America's annual coke habit could be transported in just fifteen 40-foot containers, and it takes on average five agents 3 hours to thoroughly inspect a single 40-foot container. And in addition to looking for drugs, the U.S. Customs Service is charged with monitoring compliance with more than 400 laws and 34 international treaties, statutes, agreements, and conventions on behalf of 40 federal agencies.[6]

Although the prevalence of migrant and narcotics smuggling seems to provide a compelling rationale for tightening controls along U.S. borders, aggressive border inspections in fact confront improbable odds while fostering the kinds of conditions that generate ample time and opportunity within a Mexican and U.S. border city for these illicit transfers to occur. Hardened borders also transform the cost-reward structure so that amateur crooks are replaced by sophisticated criminal enterprises and corruption issues become more pronounced. In short, the experience of the southwest border suggests that aggressive border security measures eventually contribute to problems that inspired them in the first place.

The Open Border Paradox

The United States has enjoyed the remarkable good fortune of having the oft-heralded "longest undefended border in the world" with its Canadian neighbor to the north. For much of the two nations' history, to the extent that there was a government presence along the forty-ninth parallel, it was only to collect customs duties. As a result, the 5,525-mile border can be summed up as a national boundary with no fences and a few tollgates.

In recent years, those tollgates have come under increasing pressure as cross border trade has flourished. Take the automotive industry, for example. General Motors, Ford, and DaimlerChrysler manufacture many of their car and truck parts at plants in the Canadian province of Ontario. Several times each day these parts are delivered to the assembly plants in the United States. Delivery trucks are loaded so that parts meant for specific vehicles can be unloaded and placed directly on the appropriate chassis as it moves down the assembly line. This "just-in-time" delivery system has given the Big Three a more cost-effective and efficient production process.

It has also generated a great deal of truck traffic. For example, nearly 9,000 trucks a day transited the Ambassador Bridge between Detroit, Michigan, and Windsor, Ontario in 2001.[7] At these rates, U.S. Customs officials must clear one truck every eighteen seconds. If they fall behind, the parking lot can accommodate only ninety tractor-trailers at a time. Once the parking lot fills, trucks back up onto the bridge.

The resulting pileup virtually closes the border, generating roadway chaos throughout metropolitan Windsor and Detroit, and costs the average automotive assembly plant an average of $1 million per hour in lost production.[8]

Over the past two decades, the episodic attention directed at the northern border was primarily centered on efforts to minimize any source of administrative friction that added to cost and delay of legitimate commerce. The notion of the forty-ninth parallel as a security issue is a recent phenomenon that burst into the limelight just before the millennium. The catalyst was the arrest in December 1999 of an Algerian terrorist with ties to Osama bin Laden in Port Angeles, Washington. Ahmed Ressam had arrived onboard a ferry from Victoria in a passenger car with a trunk full of bomb-making materials. Only a U.S. Customs Service official's unease with the way Ressam answered her questions prevented him from driving onto American soil. The jitters surrounding the Ressam arrest turned into near panic immediately following the attacks of September 11. Worries about the possibility of additional attacks led to the effective sealing of the border as every truck, car, driver, and passenger came under close examination. Within a day, there was a 16-hour wait at the major border crossings in Michigan and New York.[9] By September 13, DaimlerChrysler announced they would have to close an assembly plant on the following day because their supplies were stuck on the north side of the border.[10] On September 14, Ford announced they would close five plants the following week.[11] Washington quickly reconsidered its initial response and within a week the border inspection wait times returned close to normal.

The open and very limited controls exercised at the U.S.-Canada border would suggest that it was ripe for exploitation by criminals and terrorists. The reality is that the imperative to manage cross-border threats without disrupting trade, which amounts to more than $1 billion a day and the travel of 220 million people each year, has led to an extraordinary degree of cross-border cooperation. On the Vermont-Quebec border, for instance, Canadian and U.S. law enforcement officers at the federal, state, provincial, and local levels have been meeting for eighteen years to discuss their criminal cases without any formal charter. The relationships are such that participants sit together and share information in much the same way that they might at a roll call if they all belonged to the same police precinct.[12] The resultant collegiality spills over into their daily police work. In fact, local agents in Vermont or New Hampshire who are frustrated on occasion by bureaucratic obstacles to getting information or assistance from U.S. federal agencies have found that a successful end-run is to seek out their Canadian counterparts and ask them to serve as intermediaries for their requests.

In Washington state and British Colombia, U.S. and Canadian police, immigration and customs officials created a binational team in 1996 to work on cross-border crimes with local, state, and provincial enforcement agencies. The team was called the "Integrated Border Enforcement Team" (IBET) and initially focused on drug smuggling, but the portfolio later expanded to include terrorism. Following the September 11 attacks, Washington and Ottawa agreed to establish a total of eight of these IBETs along the border.[13]

The movement toward emphasizing a broader framework of binational cooperation versus focusing on the physical borderline gained impetus in 1999, when Prime Minister Jean Chrétien and President Bill Clinton formed a process of consultation labeled the "Canada-U.S. Partnership" (CUSP). The process had as its objective the reinvention of border management to support the seamless passage of legitimate flows of people and goods between the two countries.[14] Progress toward this end was somewhat halting until after September 11. With 40 percent of its GDP tied to trade with the United States, the post–9-11 closing of the border transformed the CUSP agenda into Ottawa's top priority.[15] The then Canadian foreign minister, John Manley, was dispatched to Washington to meet with the new White House director of Homeland Security, Tom Ridge. Manley found a sympathetic audience in Ridge who had just stepped down as governor of Pennsylvania. (Canada was that state's primary trade partner.) Together, they hammered out a 30–point "Smart Border Action Plan," which they announced on December 10, 2001. The preamble of the declaration declared:

> Public security and economic security are mutually reinforcing. By working together to develop a zone of confidence against terrorist activity, we create a unique opportunity to build a smart border for the 21st century; a border that securely facilitates the free flow of people and commerce; a border that reflects the largest trading relationship in the world.[16]

In dramatic contrast to the approach the United States had pursued on its southern border throughout the 1990s, Washington has concluded that with respect to its northern border its security is optimized by striving to keep the border as open as possible while working to improve cooperative binational arrangements. Efforts to harden the border along the forty-ninth parallel have been assessed to be self-defeating, not just in economic terms but also in security terms. Closing the border in the wake of a terrorist attack only reinforces the military value of engaging in such attacks. This is because it means the U.S. government ends up doing something to itself that no other world power could aspire to accomplish: It imposes a blockade on its own economy. The result is to convert a small investment in terror into massive disruption of daily life that has a clear and adverse effect on the U.S. and overall global economy. America's adversaries would undoubtedly take solace in this and recognize that the potential benefits of this kind of warfare warrant consideration.

Beyond Border Control

Embracing openness and advancing homeland security need not be an "either/or" proposition if Washington is willing to apply the lessons it has drawn from its northern border to Mexico and the broader global community. The endgame must not be about defending a line on a map, but advancing greater trilateral and global market integration while managing important safety, security, and other public policy interests. This balancing act can be accomplished by 1) developing the means to validate in advance the overwhelming majority of the people and goods that cross the border as law-abiding and low risk; and 2) enhancing the means of federal agents to target and intercept inbound, high-risk people and goods. Accomplishing the first is key to succeeding at the second since there will always be limits on the time and resources available for agents to conduct investigations and inspections. The goal must be to limit the size of the haystack in which there are most likely to be illicit needles.

Verifying legitimate cross-border flows as truly legitimate is not as fearsome a task as it might first appear. This is because aggregate border crossing numbers are misleading since so many vehicles, drivers, and people are regular customers. For instance, while there were

4.2 million recorded southwest border truck crossings in 1999, these crossings were made by roughly 80,000 trucks.[17] If we are willing to make the investment, the technologies are certainly available to identify frequent travelers as such. After undergoing a prescreening application and inspection process, vehicles can be equipped with an electronic transponder and the driver can be provided with an ATM-style identity card with encoded handprint[18] or retina information to confirm that they are who they profess to be.

Next, manufacturers, carriers, shippers, importers or exporters could be encouraged to adopt stringent internal security practices that reduce their exposure to internal criminal conspiracies and that deter criminal elements from targeting their vehicles and goods once they leave a factory, warehouse, or transshipment facility. They should also be encouraged to invest in information and tracking technologies to maintain near real-time accountability of their drivers, vehicles, and cargo from the point of origin through the final destination. Finally, they should transmit in advance the electronic information border agents need to assess their compliance with the applicable laws and regulations.

Although some in the private sector are likely to balk at these requirements, they are not radical impositions. For most modern firms, it is in their own interest to invest in the kinds of systems that provide greater levels of oversight and control throughout the international transportation process. This is because their profitability is tied in no small part to their ability to satisfy growing competitive pressures to embrace supply-chain management imperatives built around efforts to trim inventories and to meet "just-in-time" delivery schedules. Prospering in the global marketplace increasingly requires constructing virtual worldwide assembly lines with minimally stocked shelves, which, in turn, makes compulsory a degree of logistical choreography impossible just a few years ago. Given the high costs associated with cargo losses or delays, managers want guarantees that goods will arrive by the date specified in the contract. Many transportation and logistics firms are responding by embracing new tagging, tracking, communications, and information technologies that make it possible to monitor in near real time the flow of products and passengers as they move from their points of origin to their final destinations. Shipper websites, such as those developed by the Ohio-based Roadway Express, provide customers with their own personal home page where they can monitor all their active shipments aboard the company's global positioning, system-equipped trucking fleet, including their current locations and a constantly updated estimate of the expected delivery times.[19]

Security concerns are also receiving new priority in the global marketplace because rising insurance costs associated with skyrocketing cargo theft place a premium on tightening safeguards within the transportation industry. According to the National Cargo Security Council, American companies lose an estimated $12 to $15 billion a year in stolen cargo.[20] The computer industry has been particularly hard hit, with theft and insurance costs adding an estimated ten percent to the cost of the average personal computer. Sixty high-tech companies with combined annual revenues of $750 billion have responded by forming the Technology Asset Protection Association (TAPA). Founded in 1997, TAPA has identified a comprehensive set of security practices to govern the shipment of members' supplies and products. If a freight forwarder or carrier wants to do business with any of TAPA's well-heeled members, they must adopt these practices.[21]

Thus market pressures are mounting for participants in the transportation and logistics industries to embrace standards and adopt processes that can make many border-control activities redundant or irrelevant. In response to these pressures, companies are becoming better able to implement safeguards, police themselves, and provide useful and timely information necessary for public security information, which inspectors have traditionally tried to verify independently at border crossings. Theft-resistant transportation networks are more difficult for criminals and terrorists to compromise. Should there be advance intelligence of such a compromise, these information systems will make it easier to locate and interdict a contaminated shipment before it enters a crowded port or land border inspection facility; alternatively, authorities can put together a "controlled-delivery" sting operation, where the contraband is allowed to reach the intended recipient so that the appropriate arrests can be made.

Still, bringing about the kind of transformation that makes the private sector a willing and able partner in supporting a reinvented border control mission requires powerful incentives. Happily, such an incentive exists if the U.S. government is thoughtful about how new investments in transportation infrastructure are made at and near the border. Specifically, the Transportation Equity Act for the Twenty-First

Century has targeted substantial funding for major roadway improvements under the Coordinated Border Infrastructure Program.[22] As development and management plans for such projects as the "Ports-to-Plain" corridor and the I-69 NAFTA highway are drawn-up, the development of a "dedicated trade lane" should be incorporated. That is, like commuter "High Occupancy Vehicle" (HOV) lanes found around many metropolitan areas, access to a dedicated trade lane would be restricted to only those vehicles, drivers, and cargoes that participate in the new border management regime.

An additional incentive could come by moving many of the border entry inspection processes away from the physical border itself and instead consolidating them into a single trilateral "NAFTA inspection facility" and locate it on a dedicated traffic lane that leads to the border. For instance, there is an 18–mile new toll road leading from I-39 to the Mexican state of Nueva Leon via the recently constructed Colombia Bridge on the outskirts of Laredo, Texas. Why have the United States, Mexico, and Canada not agreed to grant extraterritorial legal authority within a NAFTA inspection facility placed at the start of that toll road, where trucks, drivers, and cargo could be examined by inspectors from all three countries and where each agency is allowed to enforce their respective national laws and regulations for goods and conveyances bound for their jurisdiction?

U.S. Customs has already embraced this approach in sea ports under a program Commissioner Robert Bonner has called the "Container Security Initiative." An important element of that initiative is stationing U.S. Customs inspectors overseas in loading and transshipment ports to inspect suspicious cargo before it is even loaded on a ship. Nations that agree to participate are given reciprocal privileges in U.S. ports.[23] In the North American context, the end state ideally should be to develop a single zone conducting "one-stop" arrival and departure inspections. In the case of northbound trucks from Mexico City and Monterey and southbound trucks bound for the Mexican interior, operators would have to stop just once at a location where there is plenty of space to conduct inspections and no risk of hours-long backups that now routinely plague the bridges. Once the trucks are cleared, the flow of traffic could be closely monitored by using "intelligent transportation systems" (ITS) radio frequency or GPS technologies.

But simply relocating where inspections take place is not enough. Border control agencies need to fundamentally change the way they are doing business as well. The days of random, tedious, administrative and labor-intensive border inspection systems—the bane of every legitimate international traveler and business—should be numbered. The manpower constraints inherent in traditional border-control practices guarantee their continuing inability to adequately police the surge in continental and global commerce. What is the alternative? The answer lies in a relatively new concept being developed by cyber-security experts, known as "anomaly detection."

In the computer industry, "anomaly detection" represents the most promising means for detecting hackers intent on stealing data or transmitting computer viruses.[24] The process involves monitoring the cascading flows of computer traffic with an eye toward discerning what is "normal" traffic; i.e., that which moves by way of the most technologically rational route. Once this baseline is established, software is written to detect that which is aberrant. A good computer hacker will try to look as close as possible to a legitimate user. But, since he is not a legitimate user, he inevitably must do some things differently and good cyber-security software will detect that variation, and deny access. For those hackers who manage to get through, their breach is identified and shared so that their behavior in this instance can be removed from the guidance of what is "normal" and acceptable.

In much the same way, the overwhelming majority of the vehicles, people, and cargo that move across the U.S. borders move in predictable patterns. If inspectors have the means to analyze and keep track of these flows, they will have the means to detect "aberrant" behavior. In short, "anomaly detection" of cross-border flows is possible if the regulatory and enforcement agencies whose daily tasks is to police those flows are 1) given access to intelligence about real or suspected threats, and 2) provided the means to gather, share, and mine private sector data that provides a comprehensive picture of "normal" cross border traffic to enhance their odds of detecting threats when they materialize.

If the public sector undertakes these changes, the private sector must also change its attitude about engaging in self-policing and sharing anything but the minimum amounts of relevant data with government agencies. Border control agencies have important and legitimate jobs to perform. The general public wants restrictions on the flows of contraband such as weapons, drugs, and child pornography. Immigration policies require that those entering and leaving their jurisdictions be monitored and controled. Many public health strategies aimed at managing the spread of disease require the identification and isolation of people, livestock, and agricultural products that could place the general population at risk. Safety and environmental threats connected with unsafe shipping and trucking mandate that the transportation sector be monitored. And trade rules must be enforced for trade agreements to be sustainable.

Barriers to Continental Progress

The approach to border management outlined above has started to gain some currency with respect to the U.S.-Canada border. Just before the first anniversary of the tragic attacks on New York and Washington, President George W. Bush and Prime Minister Jean Chrétien met on the Detroit-side of the Ambassador Bridge to launch an initiative dubbed the "Free and Secure Trade" (FAST) program whose purpose is to move preapproved goods across the border quickly. The two leaders also announced the expansion of a program known as NEXUS, designed to speed the flow of prescreened "low-risk" travelers across the border, along with other actions they are taking in support of the Ridge-Manley Smart Border agreement.[25] Against the backdrop of the world's busiest commercial border crossing, President Bush declared:

> With these two initiatives, we'll ensure faster movement of legal, low-risk goods, and faster travel for people crossing our borders, and we'll be able to better enhance security. Our inspectors will spend less time inspecting law-abiding citizens and more time inspecting those who may harm us.[26]

For his part, Prime Minister Chrétien asserted:

> We recognized that we could create a "smart border"—one that was not only more secure, but more efficient for trade, to permit our businesses to get back to business, to allow our nurses, engineers, and computer technicians to provide their services, and our students to attend classes. To let our communities continue planning a shared future together, secure in the knowledge that the border welcomes legitimate trade and travelers.[27]

While ample challenges remain with regard to adequate staffing, infrastructure, data management, and intelligence issues to make this "risk management" approach more capable and credible, there is clearly a consensus that measures that would have the net effect of hardening the border between Canada and the United States would be counterproductive. Meanwhile, the situation on the U.S.-Mexican border stands in marked contrast. This is not for the want of any willingness on Mexico's part. President Vicente Fox has repeatedly offered to have a no-holds-barred conversation on the future of its shared border with the United States. But there has been little enthusiasm in the post–9-11 Washington to reciprocate.

While the new homeland security imperative is cited as the rationale for change to the north, to the south, it is being proffered up to explain why the U.S.-Mexican border reform agenda has moved from the political fast track to the breakdown lane. The persistent incidence of crime, narcotics and migrant trafficking, and corruption are rallying points for advocates of "tightening-up" border enforcement. The generally unchallenged assumption is that, now more than ever, the United States needs to be committed to vigilance along the southern border.

Yet the case for fundamental reform should be even more compelling. Presumably, the combination of the new high security stakes and the acknowledgement in the Ridge-Manley agreement that hardening the forty-ninth parallel is self-defeating should create fertile ground for a thoughtful reexamination of the prevailing approach to managing the southern border. So why does this logic fail to become the prevailing one? The answer lies with the fact that the southern border is imprisoned in a legacy of immigration and drug enforcement efforts. Despite two decades of evidence to the contrary, Washington continues to see interdiction at the border as the key to successfully combating the northbound flow of illicit drugs and migrants.

It is not only Washington that has been reluctant to see the border reform agenda advanced within a broader trilateral context; Ottawa also discerns little value to joining in a comprehensive North American dialogue on border management as it does not want to have its own immediate interests (in preserving an open border) derailed by the more politically charged issue of America's relationship with its southern neighbor. Additionally, there is clearly a preference in Canada to work under the umbrella of its "special relationship" with the United States. Many in Ottawa witnessed with some angst the post-NAFTA transformation in U.S.-Mexican relations that increasingly made it difficult for Canada to pursue trade and other issues with Washington in a purely bilateral context. Anxieties over U.S.-Canadian relations being increasingly marginalized became particularly pronounced with the election of President Bush, given his ties to Mexico as the former governor of Texas and his very public friendship with President Fox. September 11 changed all that as Washington seemingly rediscovered that its largest trading partner was Canada, and its neighbor was a critical security ally it could not afford to take for granted.

In the end, there currently seems to be little appetite for pursuing a continental agenda for border management. To adopt the "smart border" agenda throughout North America would require that Washington countenance an alternative approach to dealing with the issues of illicit drugs and immigration. It would require the federal agencies, for which border enforcement has been a growth business, to acknowledge that the unintended consequence of their collective effort has been to actually make the border region more difficult to police and secure. Moreover, it would require Canada to be willing to apply its "special relationship" status with the United States toward the end of advancing the broader continental agenda versus just its bilateral one with its biggest trade partner.

Conclusion

The most important reason to get border management right is to satisfy what is arguably the most critical homeland security imperative of our time: to reduce the risk that hemispheric and global trade lanes will be exploited to smuggle weapons of mass destruction into the United States. Without a committed effort to advance a continental approach to border management, terrorists will continue to have ample opportunity to bring their battles to American streets. It is in the collective interest of the United States, Canada, and Mexico to work together to mitigate that risk.

But the impetus for challenging conventional notions of border control owes its source not just to a transformed post–9-11 threat environment, but to a long overdue response to the evolution of commercial and social patterns of interaction throughout North America that have made continental relationships more dynamic, organic, and integrated. The case against traditional border management practices, such as those pursued along the southwest border, had been already made by the close of the last century for anyone willing to look objectively at the yawning gap between enforcement rhetoric and reality. Stepped-up efforts to harden the border are a flawed, even counterproductive, approach to advancing important security and public policy interests.

Conversely, the "smart border" initiatives being embraced on the northern border hold out real promise. The outline for transformed border management is clear. It requires a risk management approach to policing cross-border flows that includes the close collaboration of the major beneficiaries of an increasingly open North American continent—the United States' neighbors to the north and the south—and the private sector. The stakes of getting this right are also clear. Transforming how the border is managed is an essential step toward assuring the long-term sustainability of hemispheric economic integration within the context of the transformed security environment of the post–9-11 world.

Notes

1. Peter Andreas, *Border Games: Policing the U.S.–Mexico Divide* (Ithaca, N.Y.: Cornell University Press, 2000).
2. Keith Philips and Carlos Manzanares, "Transportation Infrastructure and the Border Economy," in *The Border Economy* (Dallas, Tex.: Federal Reserve Bank of Dallas, June 2001): 11.
3. Field visit by the author to Laredo, Texas, August 20–21, 2001.
4. Office of National Drug Control Policy, *National Drug Control Strategy: 2001 Annual Report, Shielding U.S. Borders from the Drug Threat* (Washington, D.C.: USGPO, 2001).
5. U.S. Customs Service, "About U.S. Customs," accessed on September 6, 2002 at www.customs.gov/about/about.htm.
6. "Transport in Canada: 2001 Annual Report," Transport Canada, July 4, 2002, 73.
7. Stephen E. Flynn, "Beyond Border Control," *Foreign Affairs* 79, no. 6 (November–December 2000): 59–60.

8. U.S. Customs Service, "Border Wait Times" at major northern and southern border crossings. For current border wait-times, see www.customs. gov/travel/travel.htm.

9. Steve Erwin, "Automakers Forced to Shut Down: Parts Shortage Suspends Production," *Edmonton Journal,* September 14, 2001, F4.

10. "Parts Shortages Cause Ford Shutdown," *Associated Press,* September 14, 2001.

11. The committee is informally known as the "Leene Committee," named for its founder, James Leene, a former policeman who serves in the U.S. Attorney's Office in Burlington, Vermont.

12. Sixth Annual Canada-U.S Cross-Border Crime Forum Press Release, July 6, 2002, accessed on September 6, 2002 at www.sgc.gc.ca/Releases/e20020722.htm.

13. George Haynal, "Interdependence, Globalization, and North American Borders," in *Governance and Public Security* (Syracuse, N.Y.: Syracuse University Maxwell School, 2002), 55.

14. Authors' calculations based on statistics available at Statistics Canada, www.statcan.ca.

15. The Whitehouse Office of Homeland Security, "Action Plan for Creating a Secure and Smart Border," December 12, 2001, accessed on September 5, 2002 at www.whitehouse.gov/news/releases/2001/12/20011212-6.html.

16. Office of the Inspector General, "Interim Report on Status of Implementing the North American Free Trade Agreement's Cross Border Trucking Provisions," Federal Motor Carrier Safety Administration, MH-2001-059, (May 8, 2001), 7. Also, Statement of the Honorable Kenneth M. Mead, Inspector General, USDOT, "Motor Carrier Safety at the U.S.–Mexican Border," July 18, 2001, before the Committee on Commerce, Science and Transportation, United States Senate.

17. U.S. Immigration and Naturalization Service has already developed this technology in an "INSPASS" identification card and kiosk system for "low-risk, frequent business travelers entering the United States" at the major international airports in the U.S. and Canada. It has also set up a similar program called "SENTRI" for "low-risk frequent border commuters" at the San Ysidro and Otay Mesa, California border crossings.

18. Roadway Express homepage accessed on September 6, 2002 at www.roadway.com.

19. Telephone interview with Joseph Baker, Executive Director, National Cargo Security Council, Washington, D.C., August 2001.

20. See www.tapaonline.org/.

21. Section 1119(a) of the Transportation Equity Act for the 21st Century authorizes the Secretary of Transportation to "... establish and implement a coordinated border infrastructure program under which the Secretary may make allocations to border States and metropolitan planning organizations for areas within the boundaries of 1 or more border States for projects to improve the safe movement of people and

goods at or across the border between the United States and Canada and the border between the United States and Mexico." TEA-21 became Public Law 105-178 on June 9, 1998.

22. Robert C. Bonner, "Pushing Borders Outwards: Rethinking Customs Border Enforcement," speech presented at the Center for Strategic and International Studies, Washington, D.C., January 17, 2002.
23. Intrusion Detection Resources, accessed on September 6, 2002 at www.cerias.purdue.edu/coast/ids/ids-body.html.
24. "Summary of Smart Border Action Plan Status," Press Release, Office of the Press Secretary, The White House, September 9, 2002, www.whitehouse.gov/news/releases/2002/09/20020909.html.
25. Transcript of remarks by President George W. Bush and Canadian Prime Minister Jean Chrétien at Detroit Customs Station, Monday, September 9, 2002, www.whitehouse.gov/news/releases/2002/09/20020909-4.html.
26. Ibid.

7

WHITHER NAFTA

A Common Frontier?

GARY CLYDE HUFBAUER AND
GUSTAVO VEGA–CÁNOVAS[1]

Canada, Mexico, and the United States have reached a critical juncture in their economic and security relations. As a result of the Canada-United States Free Trade Agreement (CUSFTA) in 1989 and the North American Free Trade Agreement (NAFTA) in 1994, the three countries have seen their trade and investment relations undergo an exponential growth. With trade flows between Canada and the U.S. reaching $411 billion, and between Mexico and the U.S. reaching $263 billion in 2000, the two neighbors have consolidated their position not only as the first and second most important U.S. trading partners, but also as the leading foreign export markets for many U.S. states.[2] They also rank among the most important recipients of direct U.S. foreign investment.

In light of this commercial and investment success, it is not surprising that by early 2001 within the three countries, and especially within Canada and Mexico, many people were calling for new measures to reduce border congestion and transaction costs. Along with Mexican President Vicente Fox, some observers advocated permanent open borders and the creation of a North American Community.[3]

All this changed with the attacks of September 11, 2001. U.S. authorities imposed security measures at the borders north and south. Cross-border retail shopping and tourism plunged. Since the early post-attack weeks, the U.S. Customs Service has beefed up its staffing along the border and plans to triple the number of agents.

September 11 added a new dimension to the NAFTA project. If economic borders have been largely dismantled under the banner of free trade, security borders have suddenly become more sensitive. Unless the NAFTA countries come to grips with this new reality, the progressively higher level of economic integration achieved between 1989 and 2002 may simply come to a halt. Under a worst-case scenario—trained terrorists, armed with biological or nuclear weapons, slipping into the United States from Tijuana or Windsor—new security barriers could prove every bit as daunting to trade and investment flows as the tariffs and quotas that were negotiated away under NAFTA.[4]

In this chapter we propose an agenda for action for the three North American countries to avoid a worst-case scenario and further the economic integration in North America. We have coined this agenda for action a Common Frontier. The rationale for a Common Frontier is to reduce the risk of security threats and to channel new policy measures in a cooperative direction, if and when bad events occur. To have a chance of success, this agenda would need to accommodate the political realities of North America.

In the first part of the chapter, we briefly review the substantial achievements NAFTA members have made in their original goal of economic integration and we analyze the implications of the September 11 attacks for the future of North America. In the second part, we propose an agenda for the common frontier project in an ascending order of sensitivity, and hence political difficulty, in reaching agreement. This agenda covers three topics: border management, defense alliance, and immigration. In the final section, we outline the obstacles to a Common Frontier project but also assess the opportunities.

The NAFTA Project: Commercial and Investment Success

Canada and Mexico have a history of both policy-led and market-led economic integration with the United States, but there is no doubt that the pace of integration accelerated as a result of NAFTA implementation in 1994. Since NAFTA went into effect, trade flows

Table 7.1   Regional Trade under NAFTA, 1993–2000

	(BILLIONS OF U.S. DOLLARS)							
	1993	1994	1995	1996	1997	1998	1999	2000
U.S. Imports from Canada	111.2	128.4	144.4	155.9	168.2	170.0	198.7	229.2
U.S. Imports from Mexico	40.0	49.5	62.1	74.3	86.0	94.5	109.7	135.9
Canadian Imports from the U.S.	88.3	100.5	109.8	115.4	132.5	135.2	144.9	154.4
Canadian Imports from Mexico	2.9	3.3	3.9	4.4	5.0	5.1	6.4	8.1
Mexican Imports from the U.S.	45.3	54.8	53.8	67.5	82.0	93.5	105.2	127.6
Mexican Imports from Canada	1.2	1.6	1.4	1.7	2.0	2.2	2.9	4.0
TOTAL	288.9	338.1	375.4	419.2	475.7	500.5	567.8	659.2

Source: U.S. Department of Commerce, Statistics Canada, and SECOFI. For accuracy purposes import data is the preferred source.

between the three partners have experienced tremendous growth, surpassing the most optimistic predictions of free trade proponents. As shown in Table 7.1, between 1993 and 2000, trade in the NAFTA region increased from $289 billion to $659 billion (all money figures here are expressed in U.S. dollars) growing at an annual rate of 12.5 percent, a rate substantially higher than the average annual growth rate for world trade of 8 percent.

Total trade between Canada and the United States has more than doubled, while between Mexico and the United States it has tripled (see Table 7.1).[5] Mexico-Canada trade has also sprouted under NAFTA, despite the geographic distance and limited historic ties. Mexico has become Canada's main trading partner in Latin America and its third leading supplier worldwide. Other factors, besides CUS-FTA and NAFTA, explain part of this trade growth—notably the strong U.S. economy in the 1990s, and unilateral and multilateral trade liberalization.[6] Yet empirical studies persuasively show that CUSFTA and NAFTA were responsible for the exceptionally rapid expansion of regional trade.[7]

The tremendous growth in trade has transformed the political economy of the North American region. In the past, Mexico's export operations were almost entirely concentrated at the northern border and major interior cities—Mexico City, Guadalajara, and Monterrey. Today, most of the thirty-one Mexican states, including rural states like Aguascalientes, Campeche, Durango, and Yucatan, participate in international trade.[8] Likewise, as John McCallum has shown, all Canadian provinces have dramatically expanded their exports bound for the United States.[9] The same is true for the exports of individual U.S. states bound for Canada and Mexico.

Not only has trade boomed but also foreign direct investment (FDI) and portfolio investment have shot up. Table 7.2 shows the evolution of FDI flows among the three NAFTA countries from 1989 to 2000, divided between two subperiods, six years up to NAFTA and six years after NAFTA. Canada, Mexico, and the United States all received sizable FDI flows during the twelve-year period, but there is a striking contrast between intra-NAFTA flows in the pre-NAFTA and post-NAFTA periods. Total FDI flows between the three countries were $63 billion between 1989 and 1994; during the second period, from 1995 to 2000, total flows increased to $202 billion, more than tripling in dollar volume.

In sum, NAFTA has boosted greatly North American trade and investment. For Canada and Mexico, secure access to the U.S. market has become strategically important for their development prospects. The question is whether Canada and Mexico can be assured of this access after the events of September 11.

NAFTA, September 11, and Secure but Open Borders

History shows that stunning events can force a new perception of the world and a new set of policies. In 1941, Japan's attack on Pearl Harbor forced the American public to follow President Franklin D. Roosevelt's lead, abandon the entrenched post-World War I policy of isolationism, and adopt a new policy of active engagement in world turmoil. In 2002, the tragic events of September 11 are still being debated in the United States. President George W. Bush has called for a global war on terrorism, based on a new doctrine of preemptive strikes, and the creation of a new Department of Homeland Security with extensive powers. How these initiatives will play out remains to be seen. But the same openness that fosters economic integration is

Table 7.2 FDI Flows before and after NAFTA

(IN MILLIONS OF U.S. DOLLARS)

	FROM WORLD		FROM NAFTA COUNTRIES		FROM REST OF THE WORLD		% FROM NAFTA COUNTRIES	
	1989–1994	1995–2000	1989–1994	1995–2000	1989–1994	1995–2000	1989–1994	1995–2000
Canada	42,422	134,950	21,126	69,108	21,297	65,842	49.8%	51.2%
Mexico	49,659	64,379	26,442	42,428	23,217	21,951	53.2%	65.9%
U.S.	313,983	1,013,766	15,565	90,772	298,418	922,994	5.0%	9.0%
Total	406,064	1,213,095	63,133	202,308	342,932	1,010,787	15.5%	16.6%

Note: Mexican data from 1998–2000 is not strictly comparable to earlier data. U.S. and Canadian data from 1999–2000 is not strictly comparable with earlier data.

Source: OECD (2000) for 1989–1998 data; SECOFI (2001) for 1997–2000 Mexican data; BEA (2001) for U.S. FDI in Canada 1998–2000 and NAFTA FDI in the U.S. 1998–2000; UNCTAD for world FDI 1998–2000. Canadian data converted to U.S.\$ using exchange rates from the IMF (2002).

evidently a source of vulnerability. The United States has thus begun to adopt an array of new policies to make its domestic territory and borders more secure.

For Canada and Mexico the new security policies had shocking implications. On September 11, U.S. authorities immediately imposed security measures at the borders north and south. U.S. Customs went to a high level of alert (Level 1: sustained and intense inspection). Thereafter, automobile traffic was delayed for several hours and commercial traffic for up to fifteen hours for several days. Just-in-time manufacturers, particularly auto companies, and Canadian and Mexican goods exporters, were in crisis. By some estimates, sudden shutdowns because of parts shortages cost auto makers up to $25,000 a minute in lost production.[10]

Since those early post-attack weeks, the U.S. Customs Service has beefed up its staffing along the border. The Immigration and Naturalization Service announced plans to introduce an entry-exit system by 2003 at airports and seaports, and by 2004 at the fifty largest land entry points. This system would require visitors, including those from Canada and Mexico, to have their names recorded every time they enter and leave the country.[11]

After a period of uncertainty and delay, Canada and Mexico responded by negotiating with the United States a "Smart Borders" and a "Border Partnership Action Plan," respectively.[12] These programs aim both to secure the borders for goods and people and to keep them open. So long as the war against terrorism is conducted in the Middle East, these programs should work well. However, under a worst-case scenario, with new terrorist acts in North America, it seems doubtful that the programs announced so far will preclude the erection of formidable new security fences within North America.

The attacks of September 11—and their warning for the future—pose a big challenge to the NAFTA parties. The long-term impact of new and permanently higher levels of border security would mean much greater transaction costs that act like an added tariff on North American trade, a new tax on direct investment, and an obstacle to business and pleasure travelers. Unless the NAFTA countries come to grips with this new reality, the progressive rise in economic integration achieved between 1989 and 2002 could grind to a halt. In the next section, we outline a project to avoid a worst-case scenario and instead accelerate economic and security integration.

Agenda for Action: A Common Frontier?

For all its commercial and investment accomplishments, if NAFTA is to maintain its vitality, it needs a new vision beyond accomplishments in the realm of trade and investment liberalization. In this chapter, we provisionally propose a Common Frontier. To succeed, a Common Frontier should be ambitious enough to evoke visionary leadership, but ambiguous enough to accommodate political realities in North America. Like we have, Wendy Dobson also has called for a "Big Idea" to advance the NAFTA project—Canada and Mexico cooperate to achieve U.S. security goals, and in return the United States commits to maintain open borders even in the aftermath of an attack.[13] All three parties, meanwhile, advance the agenda of economic integration.

In our view, the Common Frontier should be the analogue of the concept during the 1980s of a European Economic Space—designed to link the European Economic Community and the European Free Trade Area (EFTA). Until the European Union that came into being with the Maastricht Treaty and absorbed most of EFTA, the final destination of the European Economic Space remained a work in progress. Similarly, the Common Frontier should be a work in progress for at least a decade to foster the closer integration of North America while preserving the essential sovereignty of each partner.

As already noted in our introductory comments, we divide the agenda into three topics, which we will discuss in what we think is an ascending order of political sensitivity: border management, defense alliance, and immigration.

Rather than dwell on bureaucratic barriers and organization charts, our discussion will address deeper ideological and cultural obstacles—the sorts of issues that will bother legislators and citizens as they contemplate the concept of a Common Frontier. If top leaders champion the concept of a Common Frontier, these bureaucratic barriers will be overcome. If top leaders do not champion the concept, no amount of effort at the negotiating table will surmount the inertia of bureaucratic resistance. We start with border management.

Border Management

The whole point of NAFTA is to eliminate economic barriers—tariffs and quotas—at the two borders. Apart from agricultural trade between Canada and its partners, and a handful of sensitive products in U.S.-Mexico trade, economic barriers have largely disappeared. Increasingly, the purpose of border inspections is to ferret out contraband (especially drugs) and provide security against hazardous merchandise.

Against this background, probably the easiest way to make progress toward a Common Frontier is to improve the mundane business of managing the two North American borders—the U.S.-Canadian border (5,525 miles) and the U.S.-Mexican border (2,062 miles). We defer the much tougher question of immigration controls to a later section.

The Smart Borders and Border Partnership Action Plan, negotiated in the wake of September 11, contemplate measures like fast-tracking precleared travelers at border points; integrated border enforcement teams staffed by Mexico-U.S. and Canada-U.S. officials; Internet-based measures to simplify border transactions for small- and medium-sized enterprises; and infrastructure investment to improve access to border crossings through, for example, new highway by-passes that avoid congested downtown streets. These are all sensible measures to secure an open border for goods and services. However, the problem with most elements of these programs (apart from fast-tracking) is that they leave the current approach to customs inspection in place and do not recognize that security demands a totally different approach.

According to Stephen Flynn, also in this book, it takes a total of three inspectors working five solid hours to thoroughly inspect a 40–foot container.[14] At the Ambassador Bridge between Detroit and Windsor, 5,000 trucks enter the United States daily, and the average time per inspection is two minutes. Virtually all the truck traffic between Canada, Mexico, and the United States crosses fewer than ten ports of entry, and these were totally congested even before September 11. It is simply not feasible to adequately expand the inspection lanes and holding areas at these ten ports to cope with the needs of security inspections.

As Flynn emphasizes, there is an alternative approach to border inspection that could better tackle security concerns while facilitating cross-border trade: Relocate intensive inspections back from the border to the plants where shipments originate and then ensure continuous surveillance from origination to destination. The normal practice for collecting tariffs and enforcing other economic regulations is to let shipments pass through the border, then clear customs at the final destination. Security, by contrast, must start at the point of origin, rather than the point of destination. This will require a host of low-tech and high-tech innovations: audited security built into production lines, akin to ISO 9000; sealed and tamper-proof containers; and continuous tracking of containers (using GPS) from origin to border to destination.

NAFTA partners already have adopted a similar approach for enforcing agricultural sanitary standards by relocating inspection and certification activity away from the border to farms and plants where agricultural produce is grown or processed. U.S. meat inspectors routinely visit Canadian packing plants and U.S. agricultural inspectors are posted at Mexican avocado orchards. The payoff is a faster trip across the border—as well as better compliance with standards. After all, it's harder to inspect a packed and refrigerated container truck than an open field or processing plant. What has been accomplished already in agriculture sets the goal for customs inspection in other segments of merchandise trade.

The United States and Canada have started a pilot program to inspect, at the Canadian port of entry, shipping containers destined for the United States that arrive from Europe at Halifax and from Asia at Vancouver. This is only a start, since the pilot program does not address the far larger volume of traffic originating in U.S., Canadian, or Mexican plants. Yet the technology exists for inspection and surveillance from point of origin to point of destination. While it may be costly to implement, especially for small firms, the bigger obstacle is gaining political assent from each North American partner for intrusive practices that entail the presence of foreign customs officials. Until that assent is forthcoming and new systems are put in place, NAFTA's future will be clouded by episodes of border strangulation, as happened after September 11.

Defense Alliance

A Common Frontier project would have to be accompanied by a new defense alliance among the three NAFTA partners. The alliance would have two purposes. First, if North America is to have a Common Frontier—implying relatively free internal movement of people, goods, and capital, but a watchful eye on arrivals from abroad—the logical corollary is strong defense for all modes of entry into the perimeter. Harmful intruders will otherwise enter at the weakest point. The second purpose is to deal with threats arising within the Common Frontier—especially threats that are organized or launched from the territory of one partner into the territory of another.

Stated so blandly, a North American Defense Alliance seems the obvious corollary to a Common Frontier. Adding to its surface appeal, a defense alliance would not involve major new deployments. The partners need not station troops nor establish airbases in each other's territory.

But there the surface appeal stops. To credibly answer the threat signaled on September 11, Canada, Mexico, and the United States would need to cooperate in new ways. Canada and the United States have maintained a close, but rather orthodox military alliance since World War II. The United States and Mexico, on the other hand, only entered a military alliance during World War II. The two neighbors were sometimes at odds during the Cold War. While President Fox supports the War on Terrorism, Mexican fervor is less than the United States might wish.

On September 6, 2001, President Fox announced, at the Organization of American States, that Mexico might withdraw from the Rio Treaty, a loose military cooperation agreement with other Latin American countries. Immediately after the attacks of September 11, Rio Treaty members, including Mexico, declared their support for the United States. Yet it remains an open question whether Mexico will in fact withdraw from the Rio Treaty and, if so, whether its withdrawal presages a defense alliance with the United States and Canada or a more neutral stance in military affairs.

Added to these differences and questions is the fact that terrorism and asymmetrical warfare call for a new kind of defense alliance. In his OAS speech, President Fox suggested that the Rio Treaty was an outdated creation of the Cold War era. After September 11—these are our sentiments, not necessarily President Fox's—the problem is not so much crushing the enemy as identifying the enemy. Identification is even more difficult when the enemy is a shifting target like Al Qaeda. Enlisting broad public support in Canada and Mexico for a sustained and intrusive campaign will not be easy. Outside the United States, the target of international terrorism is seen as Uncle Sam, standing alone. Mexico and Canada may not instantly agree that "out of status" visa holders from the Arabian Peninsula should be their concern under a defense alliance. Unless the partners entertain mutual sympathy for each other's problems, a defense alliance will not have practical significance.

Assuming these obstacles can be overcome, what would be the substance of a North American Defense Alliance? We suggest several ingredients. First, intelligence sharing is a precursor to everything else. Intelligence sharing needs to cover not only ideological terrorists, but also drug kingpins and customs smuggling rings. The most sensitive concern that impedes cooperation within NAFTA is information leakage. Drug enforcement, for which much money is at stake, is plagued by leaks. Fortunately, terrorists do not have the same kind of money as drug lords. But their use of self-contained cells—a technique pioneered by the Shining Path in Peru—makes terrorists very elusive targets.

Second, the NAFTA partners should seek agreement on circumstances that justify electronic surveillance of suspects within the Common Frontier. Federal law enforcement authorities in all three countries should be permitted to seek surveillance warrants from specially designated courts, regardless of the location or nationality of the suspect.

Third, the NAFTA partners should define circumstances when a NAFTA arrest warrant can be issued to detain a suspect anyplace within the Common Frontier.[15] The warrant should be exercisable by law enforcement officers (accredited by the partner countries) throughout North America. Persons subject to arrest under a NAFTA warrant should include suspected terrorists, drug kingpins, and certain classes of customs smugglers. Extradition proceedings for these persons should be consolidated in a single court in each country.

Fourth, the NAFTA coast guard services need to work closely—and even interchangeably—to intercept smugglers. All three countries have long coastlines with unpopulated stretches, vulnerable to contraband human and merchandise cargo. This problem is particular acute for Canada. To create an effective North American Coast Guard force, most of the funds would have to be provided by the United States, but manpower, ships, planes, and other equipment would have to be procured in proportion to the extent and intensity of coastline coverage. In other words, the United States would have to furnish a disproportionate share of funding relative to U.S. material and manpower. Even with this important fiscal and political concession, it will take a while for Mexico and Canada to accept a high level of coastal surveillance with a distinct American presence.

Immigration

A Common Frontier project must include immigration among its key elements. Special NAFTA visas for business and professional immigrants set a small precedent. In the wake of September 11, new measures were implemented to speed the border crossing of business travelers. But the most sensitive immigration issues remain to be negotiated.

Of particular interest to Mexico is the treatment accorded to migrant workers. This will be a very difficult question. Before tackling the thorny problem of migrant workers, we believe that progress can be achieved on lesser immigration questions. A useful place to start is by distinguishing between non-NAFTA visitors, and the movement of NAFTA nationals.

Non-NAFTA Nationals   For people arriving from outside the NAFTA region, the Common Frontier concept requires a shared system for excluding from NAFTA territory any non-NAFTA nationals who pose a security threat.[16] Legal immigrants are already thoroughly scrutinized before they enter, but the real problem is visitors. Annually, Canada admits about 4.4 million non-U.S. visitors, and the United States admits about 29 million non-NAFTA visitors.[17] These numbers are twenty to thirty times larger than the annual intake of legal immigrants.

Non-NAFTA nationals who threaten security can be better excluded if—in addition to the measures outlined in our discussion of border management and a defense alliance—Mexico adopts visa measures that parallel those discussed between Canada and the United States. Two principal measures should be adopted.

First, the NAFTA partners should revise their visa policies jointly with a view to synchronizing program criteria and agreeing on acceptable country lists and length of stay.[18] The three countries should seek early agreement on a common visa-free regime for the widest band of countries that all three NAFTA partners can accommodate. At the same time, each NAFTA partner should exercise greater care in issuing visas to citizens of countries for which visa-free entry has not been agreed within NAFTA. Officials in each country should have electronic access to the immigration records of its partners.

Second, NAFTA partners should create a special NAFTA force to handle all third-country (non-NAFTA) immigration controls at the individual's first airport of entry into NAFTA space. Common document and biometric identification standards should be applied. Preclearance technology is already strong enough that this method can be widely implemented without an erosion of existing controls. In fact, airport inspections are more accurate and can be more efficient than inspection at land borders, where visa and identity checks, even after September 11, remain spotty.

NAFTA Nationals   Regarding movement by NAFTA nationals, the partners should adopt three measures. First, they should create a more efficient system for handling legitimate travelers among the three NAFTA countries. The border concept negotiated between Canada and the United States contains two useful ideas: high-tech identity cards for permanent residents, using biometric identifiers, and preclearance programs for frequent travelers (known as INSPASS at airports and CANPASS—dedicated commuter lanes—at land borders).

Persons using these programs must submit to background checks and pay an administrative fee. Border crossings will be faster for these persons; meanwhile, the immigration authorities can focus their attention on unknown travelers. The same system should be extended to cover legitimate travelers arriving from Mexico.

Second, the NAFTA countries should make it easier for their citizens to retire anywhere in North America. NAFTA retirement visas should be readily available as a companion to the TN visas used by firms to relocate their employees within North America. More important, Medicare and similar health benefits should be made portable within North America. An American retired in Guadalajara should be able to spend her Medicare benefits at an approved clinic in that city. The same principle should apply to a Canadian retired in West Palm Beach or a Mexican retired in Vancouver.

Finally, and most difficult between Mexico and the United States, is the looming issue of undocumented Mexican workers. Within this category are two groups: those who already reside in the United States, a group whose number reached between 3.0 and 4.5 million in the last decade; and those who will, in the future, come to the United States to work.[19] What kind of assurances could an immigration agreement provide that both satisfies security concerns and facilitates the creation of a Common Frontier?

Future Mexican Migrants   The place to start is with the ongoing flow of migrant workers arriving in the United States. When the current recession gives way to a stronger economy, the United States should take up President Fox's challenge—put forward shortly before the September 11 attacks—to substantially enlarge the annual quota of Mexicans legally authorized to enter the United States on temporary (but renewable) work permits. In recent years, legal immigration from Mexico to the United States has numbered about 130,000 to 170,000 persons annually.[20] Illegal immigration figures are of course speculative, but the Immigration and Naturalization Service (INS) in 2001 places the annual average at about 150,000 between 1988 and 1996.[21]

The way to tackle the flow problem is to start with an expanded number of legal visas, say 300,000 persons from Mexico annually.[22]

Additional visas should be issued on a work skill basis (including un-skilled workers) and not on a family reunification basis (the domi-nant test for current visas). However—and this is where security is underlined—to obtain a temporary work permit, the Mexican appli-cant will have to undergo a background check.

Once inside the United States, temporary permit holders would need periodically to inform the Immigration and Naturalization Ser-vice, using the Internet, of their address and place of employment. Permit holders could renew their permits as long as they were em-ployed a certain number of months (say eight months) in each rolling twelve-month period, had no felony convictions, and reported regu-larly to the INS. They could apply for U.S. citizenship after a certain number of years (for example, a cumulative five years as temporary per-mit holders). In the meantime, they should accumulate public Social Security and Medicare rights, as well as any private health or pension benefits.

Coupled with this substantial but closely regulated increase in tem-porary work permits, the United States and Mexico should embark on a joint border patrol program to reduce the flow of illegal crossings. Of great concern to the United States is not only the migration of Mexican workers illegally, but also the lack of security in Mexico's southern bor-der with Guatemala and Belize, through which many illegal workers pass from Central America. The program should include features such as enhanced use of electronic surveillance, ineligibility for a temporary work permit for three years after an illegal crossing, and short-term misdemeanor detention (e.g., 30 days) in Mexico following an illegal crossing. No border patrol program will eliminate illegal crossings, but a joint program, coupled with a substantial temporary work permit initiative, could reduce the flow.

Undocumented Mexicans Resident in the United States   That leaves the question of perhaps 4 million undocumented Mexicans who live and work in the United States. We do not have a magic solution. The foundation for our tentative suggestions is the proposition that these people have made permanent homes in the United States and they are not going to pick up their lives and return to Mexico. Under a set of appropriate circumstances they should be granted residence permits with eligibility for citizenship. The appropriate circumstances we envisage have two components: a threshold relating to the total number of illegal crossings and standards for individual applicants.

First, the resident permit program would be launched when the presidents of the United States and Mexico could jointly certify that the annual rate of illegal crossings does not exceed, for example, 50,000 persons. This would entail a reduction of more than two-thirds in illegal crossings estimated in recent years. The resident permit program would be suspended in years when the presidents could not make this certification.

Second, individual eligibility would require evidence that the person resided in the United States before the announcement of the program. Otherwise, eligibility standards would parallel those for temporary work permits (discussed earlier).

Third, an applicant for a residence permit who could provide satisfactory evidence of residence in the United States before the announcement of the program would not be subject to deportation (whether or not he met other eligibility requirements) so long as he or she periodically reported a place of residence to the INS, and committed no felony after the issuance of the residence permit.

Finally, holders of residence permits would be eligible immediately for public Social Security and Medicare benefits, as well as private health and pension benefits. They could apply for citizenship after five years.

Obstacles and Opportunities for a Common Frontier Project

We have outlined the policies in border management, defense, and immigration that could make the Common Frontier project feasible. None of the measures we advocate would be easy. Indeed, most of the measures go beyond what the European Union has achieved after nearly fifty years of economic integration. The measures we suggest may not even enter the realm of political possibility unless one NAFTA partner is visibly attacked by forces that stage their operation in another NAFTA country. We contend that until elements of what we have coined a Common Frontier are put in place, the risks of a worst-case scenario and the reversal of North American integration will loom on the horizon.

We conclude with a review of the political obstacles and opportunities for something like a Common Frontier project.

Obstacles

More than ever, the United States is self-absorbed in shaping a national response to terrorism. The response has both internal and external components, and both components matter to Mexico and Canada. We start with the external component.

President Bush has announced a new preemptive strike doctrine—a historic shift in military theology. For forty years, the Cold War was guided by the strategic doctrine of deterrence. Deterrence, backed by measured retaliation, worked well in a world of stable states run by rational (if autocratic) leaders. As President Bush asserted in his speech at West Point Academy, deterrence and measured retaliation cannot be the main answer to shadowy terrorists who operate in the margins of state support. Nor can it be the main answer for rogue states bent on acquiring weapons of mass destruction (WMD) to be discharged in a battle of Armageddon proportions. For such enemies, preemptive strikes will be necessary.

Preemptive strikes seldom occupy the moral high ground of retaliatory strikes. The scope for error is large. Since strike decisions must be made on the basis of uncertain intelligence, mistakes are inevitable. Debate over a preemptive strike against Saddam Hussein illustrates the problem: Even in the case of a known and dangerous international scofflaw, critics voice many doubts. Only steadfast allies will support the United States as it implements its new strategic doctrine.

A threshold obstacle for our Common Frontier proposal is the extent of Canadian and Mexican support for preemptive strikes. Will NAFTA partners prove to be steadfast military allies? U.S. leaders will not ask Canada or Mexico to contribute special forces; but they will expect intelligence tips and they will react poorly to public criticism from NAFTA leaders. The Common Frontier project, in other words, will require robust support for the preemptive strike doctrine, not just as an abstract proposition, especially when mistakes are made.

Domestically, President Bush proposes to consolidate huge blocks of federal power into a new Department of Homeland Security. As proposed, the new department would do several things at once. It would integrate the Coast Guard, the Immigration and Naturalization Service, and the Customs Service; it would link intelligence surveillance covering thousands of suspicious individuals and groups from multiple intelligence agencies—CIA, DIA, FBI, NSA, and DEA; it would coordinate the security initiatives of states and cities; and it would initiate search and arrest warrants far more readily than established practice. The new Department of Homeland Security will potentially exercise all the powers of European ministries of interior.

How much will the domestic security forces in Mexico and Canada cooperate with the new department? Extensive cooperation may be particularly hard in Canada, which has a long history of prizing civil liberties. The media will be sprinkled with stories about offbeat, but innocent, individuals and groups that fall prey to intrusive surveillance and even arrest. But the Common Frontier project, if ever launched, could barely survive the sort of mistakes that occurred in FBI headquarters— ignoring warnings from Phoenix and Minneapolis or losing track of CIA intelligence—if the fault originated in Ottawa or Mexico City, rather than Washington D.C. Faced with this dilemma, will Canada and Mexico integrate their own intelligence and surveillance systems with the new Department of Homeland Security? In other words, will the "Homeland" eventually come to mean all of North America or just the United States? Will Canada and Mexico maintain an arms-length stance, in hopes that terrorists will head straight for U.S. soil without establishing bases north or south of the border?

In short, for the United States, the overriding obstacle to a Common Frontier project is the tentative and qualified cooperation from Canada and Mexico. One explanation for the uncertain and measured post-September 11 response by both Canada and Mexico to U.S. homeland security initiatives was concern to guard against the erosion of national sovereignty. After a time, it became apparent to both governments that some cooperation was in their national interest. The Mexican government did an about-face with a public offer to coordinate customs and intelligence gathering, while the Canadian response was less public but nevertheless proactive.[23]

While Mexico seems inclined toward closer cooperation, the political obstacles are clear. In 2000, for the first time in 70 years, the Institutional Revolutionay Party (PRI) lost control of Mexico's presidency to Vicente Fox, the National Action Party (PAN) candidate whose tenets are free enterprise and free trade. President Fox sees NAFTA as the right vehicle for new agreements on energy, immigration, and border management. Fox's agenda became even more important to Mexico after September 11, as security questions shifted U.S. attention away from North America.

In the post–September 11 setting, Mexico seeks to reaffirm its partnership in North America. Further economic integration would require contentious changes to the Constitution, particularly for the oil sector. Moreover, an enhanced security effort will cost money—when funds are badly needed for health, education, and other dimensions of Mexican life.

The 2000 election that put Fox in office also delivered a split Mexican Congress. PAN alone cannot amend the Constitution or authorize funds to embark on a Common Frontier project with the United States and Canada. But together, PAN and PRI hold 83 percent of the House and Senate votes. This means that President Fox and PAN must achieve a consensus with PRI to push further integration within North America.

Consensus is not impossible. Public opinion favors NAFTA, given the perceptible positive impact on employment and income since 1995. Meanwhile business firms, which generally endorse NAFTA, have acquired a more influential voice in the reformed political setting. Congress is sensitive to both these forces. This means the climate enables President Fox to make thoughtful North American proposals to the Mexican Congress.[24]

Opportunities

The big prize for a Common Frontier is a zone of tranquillity in North America—tranquility for people in their daily lives, for tourists, and for commerce. Terrorists will continue to strike American targets as they did in Karachi in June 2002. But a Common Frontier, if it succeeds, will make strikes in North America comparatively rare events.

September 11 will be remembered not as the beginning of a long string of internal terror, but as the wake-up call.

The Common Frontier project could be initiated either by Canada and Mexico acting jointly, or by the United States. The United States is not indifferent, but it is less motivated. If purely national responses by the Department of Homeland Security obstruct the flow of goods and people across the Canadian and Mexican borders, powerful adjacent states will fiercely protest—New York, Michigan, Washington, California, and Texas among them. This predictable reaction alone would, in time, prompt U.S. national leaders to think in cooperative terms. But a Common Frontier launched in this style depends on an unhappy sequence of action and reaction: first terrorist plans hatched in Canada or Mexico; then severe U.S. border controls; then reaction from the most seriously affected states; and finally a cooperative U.S. initiative.

By contrast, a proactive push depends on joint Canadian and Mexican initiatives. Dobson has summarized the ingredients of a "Grand Bargain": In exchange for keeping U.S. borders open, Canada and Mexico join in the sort of intensive security cooperation outlined in our paper.[25] As a bonus incentive, all three countries could claim a number of juicy economic carrots—juicy but hard to dig up. It is worth spending a few paragraphs on the carrots, because they matter to ordinary firms and people in their daily lives.

Energy cooperation is one big carrot. The core idea is to boost North American capacity for greater energy self-sufficiency as insurance against the danger that other Middle East oil suppliers might go the political way of Iraq and Iran. A subsidiary idea is to ensure that, in the event of energy super-abundance or shortage, no North American partner cuts market access or supply access to the others.

Mexico could initiate energy cooperation by both opening oil and gas exploration and electricity production and distribution to private investors, including foreign firms. This fundamental change in the Mexican Constitution would be warmly greeted by the United States. It would also help Mexico achieve its pressing need to boost electricity and gas output to satisfy its internal demand, and to boost oil exports as a source of public revenue. Moreover, energy cooperation would pay a bonus by encouraging investors to expect a higher rate of growth in the Mexican economy and therefore step up their investment plans. President Fox sees these possibilities and has taken the first steps toward reforming exclusive state control of energy production and distribution.[26]

Canada could also earn major credits in Washington by negotiating a pipeline route that brings Alaska and Alberta oil and gas to the continental United States and, at the same time, satisfies trade unions and steel suppliers on both sides of the border. Already, Canada is the single largest energy supplier to the United States (surpassing Saudi Arabia), and a new pipeline would cement the strong energy relationship.

Service markets are a second big carrot. The major markets are finance, transportation, tourism, broadcasting, entertainment, health, and education. Mexican service markets are partly open, Canadian service markets are mainly closed (an important reason why foreign direct investment in Canada has been sluggish), and U.S. service markets are mainly but not entirely open. U.S. service providers would champion a Common Frontier if open service markets were part of the bargain.

Agriculture is the third big carrot. Special features restrict agricultural trade. Two that might be addressed are phytosanitary standards and differential farm subsidy programs. The U.S. Farm Act of 2002 embedded a high level of support (about $20–$25 billion annually, amounting to about 20 percent of farm revenue) for the next six years. Canada provides somewhat less subsidy assistance (expressed as a percentage of farm revenue), and Mexico less still. Mexico has already announced a new plan of higher agricultural subsidies to address the difficult circumstances of small farmers in central and southern Mexico who stand little chance of benefiting from NAFTA liberalization. Despite the high and rising level of agricultural subsidies within North America, it might be possible to free up North American agricultural trade with a system of compensating duties to offset subsidy differences on a crop-by-crop basis. A freer market would align many if not all North American agricultural interests with the concept of a Common Frontier.

A common external tariff could be a fourth big carrot. To achieve many of the practical benefits of a common external tariff, the NAFTA partners could set a long-term goal of reducing their respective most-favored nation (MFN) tariffs to the lowest MFN level applied by

Mexico, Canada, or the United States, but each NAFTA partner would retain complete freedom to negotiate its rates in the World Trade Organization, the Free Trade Area of the Americas, and bilaterally. Rules of origin would be waived for tariff-free trade within NAFTA, provided that the exporting country did not import a significant quantity of the affected inputs at tariff rates more than one percentage point lower, for example, than the MFN rates applied by the importing country. The waiver procedure could be invoked on an annual basis by each importing firm.

As a package, these reforms would not add up to a customs union. There would be no attempt to harmonize quotas. Individual NAFTA partners could still invoke antidumping and countervailing duties and other safeguard remedies—though a concerted effort might be made to limit the scope of these episodic barriers.[27] External MFN tariff schedules would converge only gradually. Rules of origin would linger for many years. Nevertheless, from the vantage point of firms investing and trading within North America, these changes would go far toward eradicating the residual commercial borders that still separate Canada, the United States, and Mexico.

A fifth and final carrot could be closer cooperation in the financial realm—starting with financial regulation. Mexico has endured a long series of repeat bank failures. The collapse of Enron and Arthur Andersen, followed by a string of Wall Street and CEO scandals, starkly revealed the underside of U.S. finance. Mexico and the United States have both started their own clean-up acts, but more could be done in a North American context. North American regulatory task forces could usefully coordinate the reform of accounting standards and corporate governance. They could provide a voice for equivalent regulation of banks, insurance companies, pension funds, and mutual funds throughout North America.

Beyond financial surveillance, the Federal Reserve Board of Governors should welcome representatives of the Banco de Mexico and the Bank of Canada to join its key meetings. In these meetings, the representatives would participate but not vote. Staff presentations to the Federal Board should cover business conditions in Canada and Mexico. Following this initiative from the "Fed," reciprocal invitations should be forthcoming from the Banco de Mexico and the Bank of

Canada. Practical steps along these lines would establish a foundation for closer monetary cooperation over the longer term.

Viewed from Ottawa and Mexico City, as well as from Washington, these five big carrots are tantalizing but difficult. Meaningful security cooperation is not easier. "If these are the price tags of a Common Frontier," political leaders might say, "let's ride with the status quo." Optimistically, Ottawa, Mexico City, and Washington will look beyond the obstacles and grasp the historic opportunity of an integrated and secure North America.

Notes

1. The opinions expressed are the views of the authors and not their affiliated institutions.
2. According to the Embassy of Canada in Washington, D.C., Canada is the leading foreign export market for the majority of U.S. states. Some of the exceptions are Alaska, Arizona, California, Florida, Hawaii, and Idaho.
3. Robert Pastor, *Toward a North American Community* (Washington, D.C.: Institute for International Economics, 2001).
4. In October 1999, the French antiterrorist magistrate, Jean-Louis Bruguiere, personally warned Canadian authorities about the notorious Ahmed Ressam. Canadian authorities gave Bruguiere's warning scant notice—much the same treatment FBI headquarters gave to warnings they received from field offices in Arizona and Minnesota about Al Qaeda operatives. In December 1999, Ahmed Ressam entered the United States from Victoria with a carload of explosives; fortunately, an alert U.S. Customs officer apprehended him. A less happy ending in a repeat performance would severely damage North American security relations.
5. Some observers speculate that, at current rates of growth, Mexico could become within a few years the first trading partner of the United States, surpassing Canada.
6. Anne O. Krueger, "Trade Creation and Trade Diversion Under NAFTA," NBER Working Paper 7429, Cambridge, Mass.: National Bureau of Economic Research, 1999.
7. See Daniel Schwanen, "Trading Up: The Impact of Increased Continental Integration on Trade, Investment and Jobs in Canada," Toronto: C. D. Howe Institute, 1997; Enrique J. Espinosa, and Pedro Noyola, "Emerging Patterns in Mexico-U.S.Trade," in Barry Bosworth, et al. (eds.), *Coming Together?: Mexico-United States Relations* (Washington, D.C.: Brookings Institution, 1997); and Ben Goodrich, "The Effects of Trade Liberalization on North American Trade," draft, Washington D.C.: Institute for International Economics, 2002.
8. SECOFI-NAFTA Office, "Mexico a Global Partner for Trade, Investment and Growth," Mexico City: SECOFI-NAFTA Office, 2000.

9. John McCallum, "Two Cheers for the FTA: Ten Year Review of the Canada-U.S. Free Trade Agreement," in Ian L. MacDonald (ed.), *Free Trade: Risks and Rewards* (Montreal and Kingston: McGill-Queen's University, 2000).

10. Wendy Dobson, "Shaping the Future of the North American Economic Space: A Framework for Action," *Border Papers*, Commentary No. 162 (Toronto: C.D. Howe Institute, 2002).

11. Ibid.

12. See ibid.; Danielle Goldfarb and William Robson, "Good Neighbors, Better Fence: Managing the Canada-US Border in an Age of Insecurity." "Border Papers," draft, Toronto: C.D. Howe Institute, 2002; SECOFI-NAFTA Office, "Mexico a Global Partner," and *The Albuquerque Tribune*, May 1, 2002, section C.

13. Dobson, "Shaping the Future."

14. See Stephen E. Flynn's chapter, "The False Conundrum: Continental Integration versus Homeland Security."

15. For an account of the EU arrest warrant, see *Financial Times*, February 15, 2002, 3.

16. As Peter Rekai, "Immigration Policy in Canada and the US: Meeting Economic and Security Imperatives," Toronto: C.D. Howe Institute, "Border Papers," draft, April 2002, points out, Canada and the United States have very different systems for admitting immigrants as permanent residents. Canada admits about two-thirds of its immigrants based on employment criteria and one-third on family reunification grounds. The proportions for the United States are reversed. In addition, Canada has a more lenient attitude toward refugees than the United States. Fortunately, there is no need to reconcile these differences. In the security context, as Rekai emphasizes, the real problem is foreign visitors and not foreign immigrants.

17. Ibid.

18. The United States is considering a 30–day limit on foreign visitor stays. In the context of a Common Frontier, Mexico, Canada, and the United States would need to agree on the length of foreign visitor stays. See *Washington Post*, 20 March 2002, A31.

19. See Pastor, *Toward a North American Community*; and Steven Camarota, *Immigration from Mexico: Assessing the Impact on the United States* (Washington, D.C.: Center for Immigration Studies, 2001).

20. See U.S. Department of Justice, Statistics Division, *Legal Immigration, Fiscal Year 2000. Office of Policy and Planning,* Annual Report No. 6, January 2002.

21. See U.S. Immigration and Naturalization Service, "Illegal Alien Resident Population," www.ins.gov, 2001. Camarota, *Immigration from Mexico*, estimates that total legal and illegal immigration from Mexico averaged about 400,000 annually between 1998 and 2000. By implication, his figures suggest that illegal immigration in recent years was running more than 200,000 annually.

22. Raul Ojeda Hinojosa, et al., "Comprehensive Migration Policy Reform in North America: The Key to Sustainable and Equitable Economic

Integration," North American Integration and Development Center Working Paper 12, University of California, Los Angeles, August 2001, recommended a similar program.

23. *Financial Times,* October 11, 2001, as cited by Dobson, "Shaping the Future." Canada has developed a legislative framework in Bill C-36 (anti-terrorism legislation that amends ten statutes and ratifies two United Nations Conventions on the suppression of terrorism). As part of this framework, Canadian officials advanced private proposals to American officials. By December 2001, a series of initiatives surfaced in the Joint Statement of Cooperation on Border Security and Regional Migration announced by U.S. Attorney General Ashcroft and Canadian Ministers Caplan (Citizenship and Immigration) and MacAulay (Solicitor General). Several days later, Foreign Minister Manley and U.S. Homeland Security Advisor Ridge signed the Smart Border Declaration.

24. While the failed attempt at tax reform suggests that the Mexican Congress is reluctant to consider politically difficult changes, this reform was in fact extremely hard for any deputy or senator to support. The tax reform failure is not necessarily a harbinger of the Congressional stance toward other reforms.

25. Dobson, "Shaping the Future."

26. See *Wall Street Journal,* August 19, 2002, A10. Recently, Mexico had a preview of the confidence effect that could come from energy reform. In granting investment grade status to Mexican debt, Standard and Poor's cited closer integration of the Mexican economy to North America. See Carla Garcia, "Clasifican a México como país confiable," *Reforma,* February 8, 2002, 1.

27. For example, individual sectors that are highly integrated (such as automobiles or electronics) could be excluded from the scope of antidumping and countervailing duties. See Gary Hufbauer, "Antitrust and Antidumping: Forever Separate Tables?" American Antitrust Institute Conference, Washington D.C., July 1, 2002.

8

THE REBORDERING OF NORTH AMERICA?

Implications for Conceptualizing
Borders after September 11

THOMAS J. BIERSTEKER

When the territory of the United States was directly struck by a pre-meditated attack planned from outside of its borders for the first time since World War II, the initial impetus of the U.S. government was to protect the territorial homeland, to close its borders, and to provide security for its public. That is precisely what it did on September 11, 2001. It grounded all aircraft and virtually sealed its borders with both Canada and Mexico. In effect, as Stephen Flynn put it in his contribution to this book, the United States imposed a costly embargo on itself.

This immediate reaction is not at all surprising. The very existence of the modern, Weberian state is legitimated by its ability to protect its citizens from attacks from outside its boundaries and to provide security and order within the territorial space defined by its borders. These are the core, traditional security functions of the state. However, one of the most basic practical and theoretical problems faced by the U.S. in the immediate aftermath of September 11 was how to balance competing, but legitimate state security functions. How could the need for physical security protection from violence be balanced by the need to maintain an open economic and commercial border that promised both economic security and the benefits of a continuation of expanded commerce? The authors included in this book grapple with the potential tensions between these different forms of security.

The narrow pursuit of physical security and the protection from violent harm could undermine the pursuit of economic security and the provision of basic material needs. The inability to provide for basic economic security could, in turn, prove to be destabilizing politically for both Mexico and Canada, generating new forms of potential security threats to the United States.

General Conclusions

There are several general, synthetic observations that can be made following a reading of the essays in this book. First, it is striking, although not terribly surprising, to note how much scholars writing from both Canada and Mexico share a common perception of asymmetrical interdependence with the United States. Accompanying this perception is the common conviction that it is they who must adapt. Both Canada and Mexico also share common sensitivities and vulnerabilities to U.S. practices and policies, as illustrated in the chapters by Stephen Clarkson and Louis Pauly on Canada and by Athanasios Hristoulas and Mónica Serrano on Mexico. Both countries realize that innovations and initiatives in immigration, trade, and security policies are likely to emanate primarily from the United States. Canada and Mexico can try to influence U.S. policy, but they are more likely to be forced to adapt to and accommodate themselves to U.S.-initiated policies regarding their shared borders. The Mexican predicament—"so far from God and so close to the United States"—seems increasingly to be shared by colleagues north of the U.S. border, as indicated when Peter Andreas refers to Pierre Elliot Trudeau's comment about "sleeping with an elephant."

Second, and related to the first point, there is an apparent convergence of views among Canadian and Mexican observers that further moves toward integration and policy harmonization in North America need to be accompanied by a greater institutionalization of governance in the region. This is an idea articulated not only by Gary Hufbauer and Gustavo Vega-Cánovas, the book's strongest advocates, for deepened North American integration, but is also contained in the chapters by Hristoulas and Clarkson. Each of the latter would like to see greater institutionalization of North American integration, with legitimate, representative, and more accountable institutions of governance in place. This form of governance, requiring new regional institutions, is dramatically different from the simple acceptance of U.S. hegemony by Canada and Mexico. While both Clarkson and Hristoulas are acutely aware of the asymmetrical relationship between the United States and each of its neighbors, both also desire the development of a more representative and institutionalized form of regional governance.

Third, another conclusion contained in several of the chapters in this book is that Canada traditionally precedes Mexico when it comes to policy initiatives and innovations with Washington. Mexico typically follows Canada a few years later with similar, though often less generous, policy arrangements. This was true of the defense arrangements negotiated during World War II, as described in chapter 3 by Mónica Serrano. Similarly, in the negotiation of free trade agreements, the U.S.-Canada free trade agreement preceded the inclusion of Mexico by more than five years. More recent, the discussion and introduction of the concept of "smart borders" has been initiated in the first instance with Canada, with a delayed and more limited extension to the U.S.-Mexico border.

Fourth, powerful economic actors, with strong interests in the continuation and development of North American regional integration, are likely to play an important role in ensuring that physical security concerns do not displace economic and commercial ones. There have been clear winners (and losers) from North American integration to date, and the winners learned a powerful lesson about the adverse consequences of the U.S. turning the pursuit of security into a new kind of trade barrier after September 11, 2001. Major economic interests on all sides of the borders—in the United States, Canada, and Mexico—will strive to ensure that the pursuit of absolute physical security does not derail the advantages of expanded trade. According to Pauly in Chapter 5, as well as in the chapters by Andreas, Clarkson, Hufbauer and Vega-Cánovas, and Hristoulas, the imperatives of economic integration appear to explain a great deal of policy continuity in the effort to maintain economic openness.

Leadership and the articulation of a vision for North America ultimately will play significant roles in determining the nature of the borders that separate the countries of the region. That is the importance of Hufbauer and Vega-Cánovas' largely prescriptive essay. The presence of a vision for the future can guide policymakers through the uncertain terrain of hard-to-predict political contingencies and resist (or redirect) the pull of powerful economic interests. The apparent ascendance of pragmatists in both Canada (John Manley), and in Mexico (Jorge Castañeda), as described in the chapters by Pauly and Serrano, suggest that there is a leadership that is prepared to articulate and move forward with an agenda to maintain the balance between physical and economic security. Pauly's prescription for the "right" kind of border, with shared security and an open regional economy, but protection (at least for Canada) from being lowered to U.S. social protection standards, presents an alternative prescriptive vision of the future. Pauly aligns himself with Clarkson's normative agenda to try to build a "better" America north of the U.S.-Canada border.

Fifth and finally, there increasingly appears to be an inexorable, even if uneven, movement toward the introduction of "smart borders." As Flynn elaborates in chapter 6, the movement to smart borders entails the prescreening of people and vehicles, increased use of tracking technology to follow the movement of goods, the development of theft-resistant, secure transportation networks, the physical movement of immigration, border, and container inspections to locations removed from the actual border, and the increased use of anomaly detection technologies to identify departures from the norm for detailed investigation. This trend toward the introduction of smart borders appears to be driven primarily by U.S. security concerns and by the interests of major U.S.-based firms that have reorganized their production over the course of the past decade to take advantage of increasing North American economic integration. Flynn forcefully argues that increased infrastructure investments in border security could also have important commercial spin-offs and economic benefits over the longer term (just as the interstate highways program did in the United States under President Dwight Eisenhower, when facing a different, Cold War security threat in the 1950s).

Implications for the Meanings
of Borders and Boundaries

What are some implications of these developments for how we think about and conceptualize the meanings of borders and boundaries? To begin, we need to move away from nineteenth-century conceptions of borders and boundaries where they are viewed as clear, unproblematic lines printed on maps; conceived of as physical barriers that sharply demarcate different political entities; and imagined as protective shields that provide tight seals around their inhabitants. Such boundaries have never actually existed in practice. They are figments of the conception of territory associated with the sovereign state of the Westphalian ideal. That idealization consists of a sovereign state with clear and unchallenged lines of legitimate political authority, with a clearly defined territorial space delimited by sharply identified boundaries, and containing a population that shares an unproblematic identity as a people. In this traditional conception, states are like containers and borders delimit their contents.

At the end of the nineteenth and beginning of the twentieth century, there was an obsession with physical possession and control of territory in the scholarly literature, in policy pronouncements, and in the popular imagination. Control over physical territorial space was vital for a scholar-practitioner like Halford Mackinder.[1] Assumptions about the virtues and benefits of territorial acquisition remained predominant until Norman Angell forcefully challenged them in 1910, with the publication of the first edition of *The Great Illusion*. Angell identified how widespread these views were at the turn of the century in both Britain and Germany, and he defined the "great illusion" as the idea that territorial acquisition would provide a basis for prosperity and affluence.[2] For Angell, territorial conquest and acquisition were futile, since the conqueror acquired liabilities along with the assets of the conquered populace. He contended that the basis of wealth was not to be found in the physical possession of territory, but in how that territory was used.

During the middle decades of the twentieth century, when the nation-state emerged as the predominant state form and the principle of sovereign nonintervention was widely proclaimed (if not always practiced), the boundaries between states became increasingly sharply drawn. The Covenant of the League of Nations in 1919 bound its members to respect the territorial integrity of its members, while the Charter of the United Nations in 1945 similarly asserted the principle of nonintervention in the affairs of member states.[3] The movement of peoples, so widespread during the late nineteenth century, became increasingly difficult as state after state raised the barriers to entry. In the economic realm, national capital controls and international monetary agreements protected national currencies from the destabilizing influences of international market forces.[4] Elaborate alliance networks guaranteed the security and territorial integrity of their members, whether they were allied with the United States or the Soviet Union.

It was only after the advent of the nuclear age that states reluctantly began to recognize their strategic vulnerability, and their increased reliance on the symbolic territorial protection provided by nuclear deterrence. During the last fifty years, major powers have grown accustomed to (if not comfortable with) this vulnerability. American efforts to develop a national missile defense shield at the beginning of the twenty-first century should be interpreted as an attempt to reconstruct a hard and virtually physical boundary around the United States, a development that has prompted strong objections from allies and potential adversaries alike. It is unclear what its successful deployment would mean for North America. If successful, it might be extended to Canada and Mexico, under the umbrella of perimeter security. Alternatively, in an effort to maintain sovereign identity on the part of either or both countries, the situation might remain more ambiguous.

By the end of the twentieth century, both the salience of physical territory and the significance of borders appeared to be on the decline in many issue domains, with the only major exceptions involving the movement of people and prohibited goods such as drugs. There was a subtle shift away from the state as the spatial unit within which problems are assumed to be most appropriately confronted, a development we have clearly seen in North America.[5] Increasingly, it is the control of networks—finance, information, raw material flows, cyberspace, investment, and transportation—that is more important than control of physical, territorial space. This is an observation made by geographers and political scientists alike.[6] However, as sociologist Saskia Sassen has reminded us, all transactions take place on some territorial space, but the precise location of those transactions is increasingly ambiguous, and they tend to be located in different places for different purposes.[7]

Beyond changes in the salience of territory, the meaning and significance of boundaries also had changed by the end of the twentieth century. With the expansion of interdependence, innovations in communications and information technologies, and the advent of globalization, political geographers started "raising questions about the changing nature and function of boundaries."[8] Political theorist Julie Mostov has distinguished between "hard" and "soft" boundaries to describe the phenomenon, arguing that a real alternative to the traditional discourse of external sovereignty and hard borders "would be to 'soften' the boundaries of the state and radically rethink notions of internal sovereignty, self-determination and citizenship rights."[9]

Late twentieth-century increases in the flows of finance, goods, information and, in some high-technology sectors, even of people, have rendered boundaries increasingly porous or "soft." The tendency toward the increased porosity of borders has been resisted by state actors throughout the world, just as it has by some substate actors located within North America. The pattern is by no means consistent or uniform across different functional activities. It is still much easier for finance to move across political boundaries than for people to move across them. Nevertheless, the important point is that the porosity of the border has varied across issue, time and space.

One of the most important questions about the aftermath of September 11 is whether the increased porosity of the North American borders in recent decades would continue after the attacks. The immediate reaction of some observers was that hard, traditional borders would be back—and back with a vengeance. As Andreas points out in Chapter 1, this was particularly evident among political interest groups like the Federation for American Immigration Reform (FAIR), who used the heightened anxiety immediately following September 11 to pursue their agenda on a single issue. However, much of the evidence is not yet in on how much borders are actually "back" (whatever that means precisely). The introduction of the concept of smart borders could be an important way to maintain important aspects of economic openness, while at the same time providing for enhanced security. As described briefly above and as elaborated in Stephen Flynn's chapter in this book, the concept of smart borders employs a combination of technological advances, administrative reforms, and adjustments of the physical location of the border to maintain security with openness. Preinspection arrangements at major container ports located across the globe moves the control authority away from the actual territorial border to a critical point in the network of global transportation systems. Similarly, reliance on commercial air carriers for the processing of vital passenger information for immigration authorities and preinspection at locations removed from the immediate border area move the locus of control to a different location. Thus, borders should no longer be thought of in literal terms as the lines that sharply divide different polities on the map. Rather, they should increasingly be thought of in functional terms, as lines that demarcate for some purposes, but not all. As John Ruggie has usefully suggested, there has been an unbundling (or uncoupling) of territory and political authority.[10]

One of the implications of post–September 11 developments in North America for our thinking about borders and boundaries is that the meaning of the line drawn to define the border is not fixed—it is socially constructed by the practices of state and nonstate actors. The border is historically a line, demarcating authority domains across which things change, sometimes dramatically. Traditionally, the border has been a point where inspections take place. Protectionist, closed states during the middle part of the twentieth century controled, or at least attempted to control, large numbers of transactions (of goods, people, currencies, and even ideas). During the latter part of the twentieth century, most states lifted controls on the movement of goods, currency, and ideas—but not people. Therefore, the range of things controled, or over which states have attempted to assert their authority, changes over time. Simultaneously, the physical location of inspections—or points at which the state asserts its control—varies. Thus, when thinking about the nature of borders and boundaries, the important point to remember is that the border changes in two dimensions: both over what it attempts to control, and where it attempts to assert its controling authority. Its salience and meaning vary according to the ease with which different types of goods and services are allowed across it (the porosity of the border), and it varies according to the actual physical location at which the state attempts to assert its authority.

Perhaps the most significant aspect of the line drawn to demarcate the border is not the actual physical location of the inspection of goods and people, but the jurisdiction under which the inspections take place. There are often competing and/or conflicting claims of legal jurisdiction in any particular case, but the changing meaning of the border may be captured best by the idea of moving from a physical line of demarcation—the traditional nineteenth-century view—to a legal jurisdiction, defined by practices of authority claims by states (and some nonstate actors) and recognized as legitimate by other states and nonstate actors.[11] In the final analysis, state jurisdictional claims of authority define the operational meaning of the border, both how hard or how soft it is, and precisely where (in legal, not physical space) the authority is exercised. Not only are the issues over which states claim authority (and the need for control) variable, but the location of the assertion of that control also changes.

Since the nature of the most important contemporary global security threat is a networked one emanating from Al Qaeda, it is appropriate that a security response to the threat also be designed in network terms. The emphasis in the smart border discussion on strategic interventions for different points in the networks of transportation, information, communications (or like the counterterror effort to freeze terrorist finances) are illustrations of efforts to provide a networked response to a networked threat to security. As political economists and geographers have suggested, recent changes in the organization of global finance have "rendered ambiguous" the traditional territorial imagery of international political economy.[12] Control over flows and networks is becoming more important than hierarchical control over physical territorial space.[13]

In addition, the emergence of the "region-state"—economic zones with integrated industrial investment and information systems that straddle national boundaries in an increasingly borderless world—is yet another manifestation of the blurring of traditional conceptions of territoriality.[14] This blurring of territoriality is apparent in the intense and growing regional interdependence between the United States and both Canada and Mexico. The recession in Mexico following the peso crisis in the mid-1990s had major short-term effects on the regional economy of the American southwest, and in some spheres of activity, what happens in Mexico City has become more important for Los Angeles than what happens in Boston.

Alternative Futures

In their collective effort to think about the potential outcomes and alternative futures facing the countries of North America and the borders that divide them, our authors survey three broadly different analytical possibilities—from the creation of an isolated, unilateral, "fortress America" at one end of the spectrum, to the dissolution of borders and "accelerated integration" of the three principal countries of North America at the other end of the spectrum. As Clarkson points out in Chapter 4, the formation of a "fortress America," a gated community that excludes both Canada and Mexico, is a real possibility and an object of genuine concern to colleagues north and south of the U.S. border. This is the scenario of U.S. unilateralism "run amok," with potentially devastating consequences for both Canada and Mexico facing exclusion from access to the U.S. market.

At the other extreme is the possibility that the attacks of September 11 will provide an impetus for an acceleration of recent patterns (at least over the course of the past decade) of integration of North America, in a "Europeanization" of borders and an emulation of European efforts at regional integration. This is one of the scenarios explored and encouraged by Hufbauer and Vega-Cánovas in their joint contribution in chapter 7. Within this broad category of greater integration, there is a significant range of possibilities, from the "Shengenization" of North American borders (considered by Hufbauer and Vega-Cánovas, as well as by Andreas) and the construction of a North American security perimeter, to the less intensive form of integration envisioned (and normatively preferred) by Clarkson, with the promise of a porous but not vanishing border. Among Canadian and Mexican objections to the scenario of an acceleration of regional integration is that it would lead to a potential loss of sovereign identity. Clarkson, in particular, does not want to see full harmonization of practices and policies to U.S. standards, but would prefer raising all standards, by whatever policy means, as a general goal. Other objections raised include a concern about a potential slowing of the introduction of smart borders (as discussed by Flynn in chapter 6), and the "Mexicanization" of the US-Canada border (as discussed by Andreas in chapter 1).

An alternative to either of the two preceding scenarios (of fortress America or accelerated integration of North America) is the possibility that one outcome of the attacks of September 11 will be the more complete integration of Canada, to the exclusion of Mexico. This appears to be one of Hristoulas's principal concerns when he suggests in chapter 2 that this idea fits a long-standing pattern and has Canada's explicit support. That is, a "smart," barrier-free border should be introduced to the northern U.S. border as soon as possible. Eventually, this type of border could be introduced to the southern border when Mexico is more developed and ready for a "Canadianization" of its border with the United States. That would imply that the hard border of Mexico would need to be pushed southward, to its borders with the countries of Central America. Not surprisingly, none of the contributors sees the obverse case (closer integration with Mexico to the exclusion of Canada) as a likely alternative.

Over the longer term, the likelihood of any of these three different scenarios unfolding will depend very much on contingencies of a very uncertain future. First, if and/or when there is another terrorist attack on the U.S. territory and population, it will affect dramatically the assessment of the threat from global terrorism. Second, and more important, if another terrorist attack on U.S. territory emanates from the territory of either Canada or Mexico, it will affect significantly the revised assessment of threat and the unfolding possibilities for the borders (both what should be controled and where it should be controled). Efforts to balance physical security with economic openness could tip dramatically away from openness, as Hufbauer and Vega-Cánovas, as well as Andreas warn. Third, and finally, if the United States acts unilaterally, and with disastrous results, against Iraq, both Mexico and Canada could turn away from closer identification with the United States for fear of becoming targets for expanded terrorist attacks themselves.

Much research remains to be done on the changing meaning of borders and boundaries in North America. The essays in this book take us a long way toward beginning the important conceptual and empirical work needed to comprehend their meaning. The terrorist attacks on the United States on September 11, 2001, forced all of us in North America to rethink many of our assumptions about the nature of security at the beginning of the twenty-first century. The residents of the United States, Canada, and Mexico no longer live in relative isolation from the rest of the world. It is important that we come to terms with our changed circumstances and develop creative ways to provide for security, without sacrificing the democratic ideals that legitimate our polities.

Notes

1. Sir Halford J. Mackinder, "The Geographical Pivot of History," *The Geographical Journal* 23, no. 4 (1904): 421–444.
2. Norman Angell, *The Great Illusion: A Study of the Relation of Military Power in Nations to their Economic and Social Advantage* (New York and London: G. P. Putnam's Sons, The Knickerbocker Press, 1910): 30–31.
3. Alan James, *Sovereign Statehood: The Basis of International Society* (London and Boston: Allen and Unwin, 1986).
4. John G. Ruggie, "International Regimes, Transactions and Change: Embedded liberalisation in the Post-war Economic Order," *International Organization*, 36, no. 2 (1982): 379–415.
5. Alexander B. Murphy, "International Law and the Sovereign State System: Challenges to the Status Quo," in George J. Demko and William B. Wood (eds.), *Reordering the World: Geopolitical Perspectives on the Twenty-First Century* (Boulder, Colo.: Westview, 1999): 235.
6. For observations by geographers, see John Agnew and Paul Knox, *The Geography of the World Economy: An Introduction to Economic Geography* (New York: Routledge, Chapman and Hall, 1994); and Alexander B. Murphy, "Political Geography," in N. D. Smelser and P. B. Baltes (eds.), *International Encyclopedia of the Social and Behavioral Sciences* (Amsterdam: Pergamon, 2001). For observations by political scientists, see Timothy W. Luke, "The Discipline of Security Studies and the Codes of Containment: Learning from Kuwait," *Alternatives* 16, no. 3 (1991): 315–344; and Susan Strange, *The Retreat of the State: The Diffusion of Power in the World Economy* (New York: Cambridge University Press, 1996).
7. Saskia Sassen, *Losing Control? Sovereignty in an Age of Globalization* (New York: Columbia University Press, 1996).
8. Murphy, "Political Geography," 13.
9. Julie Mostov, "Rethinking Sovereignty, Democracy and the Politics of National Identity," paper presented at the Watson Institute for International Studies conference on "Whose Self-Determination:

Agency and Amnesia in the Disintegration of Yugoslavia," Brown University, February 4–5, 2000, 6–7.

10. John G. Ruggie, "Territoriality and Beyond: Problematizing Modernity in International Relations," *International Organization,* 47, no. 1 (1993), 171.

11. Rodney Bruce Hall and Thomas J. Biersteker, *The Emergence of Private Authority in Global Governance* (Cambridge, U.K.: Cambridge University Press, 2002).

12. Stephen J. Rosow, "On the Political Theory of Political Economy: Conceptual Ambiguity and the Global Economy," *Review of International Political Economy* 1, no. 3 (1994): 465–488; Strange, *Retreat of the State*; Stephen J. Kobrin, "Beyond Symmetry: State Sovereignty in a Networked Global Economy," in John Dunning (ed.), *Governments, Globalization and International Business* (Oxford, U.K.: Oxford University Press, 1997).

13. Timothy W. Luke, "The Discipline of Security Studies and the Codes of Containment: Learning from Kuwait," *Alternatives* 16, no. 3 (1991): 315–344.

14. Kenichi Ohmae, *The End of the Nation State: The Rise of Regional Economies* (New York: Free Press, 1995): 79–82.

About the Authors

Peter Andreas, Assistant Professor, Department of Political Science and Watson Institute for International Studies, Brown University. Peter Andreas is the author of *Border Games: Policing the U.S.-Mexico Divide* (2000), co-author of *Drug War Politics: The Price of Denial* (1996), co-editor of *The Illicit Global Economy and State Power* (1999), and co-editor of *The Wall Around the West: State Borders and Immigration Controls in North America and Europe* (2000). Other writings include many scholarly and general audience articles, a congressional report, and testimonies before the U.S. Senate and the U.S. House of Representatives. He was previously an academy scholar at the Harvard Academy for International and Area Studies, an SSRC-MacArthur Foundation Fellow on International Peace and Security, and a research fellow at the Brookings Institution. He received his Ph.D. from Cornell University and his B.A. from Swarthmore College.

Thomas J. Biersteker, Henry R. Luce Professor of Transnational Organizations, and Director, Watson Institute for International Studies, Brown University. Thomas J. Biersteker is the author, editor, co-editor or co-author of six books, which include *State Sovereignty as Social Construct*, co-edited with Cynthia Weber (1996); *Argument without End: In Search of Answers to the Vietnam Tragedy*, co-authored with James G. Blight, Robert K. Brigham, Robert S. McNamara, and

Herbert Y. Schandler (1999); and *The Emergence of Private Authority in Global Governance,* co-edited with Rodney B. Hall (2002). He is also a co-author of *Targeted Financial Sanctions: A Manual for Design and Implementation* (2001). Professor Biersteker has served as a consultant to the United Nations, World Bank, World Health Organization, U.S. Department of State, and a number of private sector corporations. He currently serves on editorial advisory boards for six presses and journals. He is an honorary fellow of the Foreign Policy Association, a member of the Council on Foreign Relations, and is the chair of the Social Science Research Council's Global Security and Cooperation Committee. Professor Biersteker received his doctorate from the Massachusetts Institute of Technology.

Stephen Clarkson, Senior Professor of Political Economy, University of Toronto. Stephen Clarkson is the author of *Canada and the Reagan Challenge,* a 1982 prize-winning study of the conflict between the Canadian government and the Reagan White House over such issues as Pierre Trudeau's National Energy Policy. In addition, international audiences know his co-authored two-volume biography of Pierre Trudeau, *Trudeau and Our Times* (1990 and 1994). His latest work, *The Contested State: Canada under Globalization,* was published in 2002 by the University of Toronto and Woodrow Wilson Presses. Professor Clarkson has been a Jean Monnet Fellow at the European University Institute, where he studied the European model's relevance to North American integration, and a research fellow at the Woodrow Wilson Center, where he worked on NAFTA's impact on Canada. A Rhodes Scholar at Oxford University, he received his doctorate from the Sorbonne.

Stephen E. Flynn, Senior Fellow, National Security Studies, Council on Foreign Relations. Stephen Flynn directs a multi-year project at the Council on Foreign Relations, "Protecting the Homeland: Rethinking the Role of Border Controls," and is also a commander in the U.S. Coast Guard, as well as a member of the Coast Guard Academy's Permanent Commissioned Teaching Staff. Dr. Flynn served in the White House Military Office during the George H. W. Bush administration and as a director for global issues on the National Security Council staff during the Clinton administration. Among his recent publications are "America the Vulnerable" in *Foreign Affairs* (Jan./Feb. 2002) and "The Unguarded America," which appears in a collection of essays on the September 11 attacks published by PublicAffairs Books. He has been a guest scholar in the Foreign Policy Studies Program at the Brookings Institution and an Annenberg Scholar-in-Residence at the University of Pennsylvania. He graduated from the U.S. Coast Guard Academy and served twice in command at sea. Dr. Flynn received a M.A.L.D. and Ph.D. from the Fletcher School of Law and Diplomacy, Tufts University.

Athanasios Hristoulas, Professor of International Relations at the Instituto Tecnológico Autónomo de México (ITAM). Athanasios Hristoulas received his Ph.D. from McGill University in 1996. Before moving to Mexico from Canada, he was the Military and Strategic Studies Post Doctoral Fellow at the Norman Paterson School of International Relations, Carleton University. His research interests include civil-military relations, Mexican defense and national security policy, and Canada-Mexico relations. He has previously published in such journals as the *Journal of Politics, Etudes International, Comercio Exterior,* and *Foreign Affairs en Español.* His most recent publications include an edited volume, *Las Relaciones civico-militar en el Nuevo orden internacional* (2002), and a book chapter, "Good Governance in the 21st Century" in *The State, Interest Groups and Governance* (2002).

Gary Clyde Hufbauer, Reginald Jones Senior Fellow at the Institute for International Economics in Washington, D.C. Gary Hufbauer was formerly the Marcus Wallenberg Professor of International Finance Diplomacy at Georgetown University (1982–1992); deputy director of the International Law Institute at Georgetown University (1979–1981); and the deputy assistant secretary for international and investment policy of the U.S. Treasury (1977–1979). He has written extensively on international trade, investment, and tax issues. He is co-author of *World Capital Markets: Challenge to the G-10* (2001); *NAFTA and the Environment: Seven Years Later* (2000); *NAFTA: An Assessment* (1995); and *Economic Sanctions Reconsidered* (2d ed., 1990).

Louis W. Pauly, Professor of Political Science and Director, Center for International Studies, University of Toronto. Among Louis Pauly's publications are *Governing the World's Money* (co-editor and co-author, 2002); *Democracy beyond the State? The European Dilemma and the Emerging Global Order* (co-editor and co-author, 2000); *The Myth of the Global Corporation* (co-author, 1998); *Who Elected the Bankers? Surveillance and Control in the World Economy* (1997); *Choosing to Co-operate: How States Avoid Loss* (co-editor and co-author, 1993); and many shorter monographs, journal articles, and book chapters. He is on the editorial boards of *International Organization,* the *International Studies Quarterly,* and the *Review of International Political Economy.* A graduate of Cornell University, the London School of Economics, New York University, and Fordham University, he has held management positions in the Royal Bank of Canada and served on the staff of the International Monetary Fund.

Mónica Serrano, Research-Professor at El Colegio de México and Research Associate at the Center for International Studies, Oxford University. Mónica Serrano has published extensively on Mexican politics, civil-military relations, and the International Relations of Latin America. Her most recent publication is *Transnational Organized Crime and International Security: Business as Usual?* (co-edited with Mats Berdal, 2002). Forthcoming titles include *The Privatization of Violence in Latin America* and with Louise Fawcett ed., *Regionalism's "Third Wave": The Challenge of the Americas.* She received her doctorate from Oxford University.

Gustavo Vega-Cánovas, Professor, Center for International Studies, El Colegio de México. Gustavo Vega-Cánovas has written extensively on U.S.-Mexican economic relations and North American integration. This includes *Unfair Trade Practices and Dispute Resolution Mechanisms in Free Trade Agreements of the Americas: The Experience of North America and Chile* (2001, in Spanish), and "NAFTA and the EU: Toward Convergence?," in *Regional Integration and Democracy: Expanding on the European Experience* (ed., Jeffrey J. Anderson, 1999). Professor Vega-Cánovas has been a member of five binational panels under Chapter 19 of the North American Free Trade Agreement (NAFTA). He is a member of the National System of Researchers (SNI in Spanish) of Mexico's Education Ministry. In addition to Brown, Professor Vega-Cánovas has been a visiting professor at several other universities, including Yale, Duke, the University of North Carolina at Chapel Hill, and the University of Washington at Seattle. He holds both a law degree and a Ph.D. in political science from the National Autonomous University of Mexico and Yale University, respectively.

Index